# tHE MURRAY
# collection
# of glass

# TURN of THE CENTURY glass

# THE MURRAY collection of glass

edited by
Philip D. Zimmerman

with an introduction by
Paul V. Gardner

The Currier Gallery of Art
Manchester, New Hampshire

Distributed by
The University Press
of New England
Hanover, New Hampshire

Typeset and printed by Acme Printing Company, Inc.

Photography by Bill Finney

Designed by Carl Zahn

Cover:

*Selection from The Murray Collection of Glass,* late 19th to
early 20th century. Wide-brimmed bowl (cat. no. 221), blue
vase (271), wire vase (282), shell compote (239), red vase
(296), cookie jar (200), cameo jar (7), Plated Amberina
pitcher (161) and "Morgan" vase (139).

# CONTENTS

# acknowledgments

The author wishes to acknowledge the Murrays —
Sophie, Albert, and Priscilla — for their respective
contributions in assembling, donating, and sup-
porting this splendid collection of glass that
through their great generosity is now available to
many other lovers of glass to appreciate and
enjoy. In addition, he wishes to note the invaluable contributions of Dorothy-Lee Jones of The
Jones Gallery and Nancy O. Merrill of The
Chrysler Museum who, along with the staff of
The Currier Gallery of Art, helped make this publication possible.

PAUL V. GARDNER


Roland and Marian Sallada have been devoted
friends for many years. Their willingness to share
a knowledge and love for the arts has been a
great source of assistance and pleasure. This catalogue is dedicated to them.

PRISCILLA MURRAY

# foreword

For those who pursue it diligently and with passion, collecting is a great adventure. The discovery of a new acquisition is an occasion for rejoicing. A collection is often the unique and distinctive expression of the individual who guided its formation, the hallmark of a sensitive and questing personality. The collector who ignores dry historical criteria and the whims of current fashion in favor of a very personal response to individual works of art also engages in a creative act as significant as the objects which are the reason for selection.

Sophie Murray was such a collector. She started collecting in the mid 1940s while living in Middleton, Massachusetts, with her husband Albert who owned and operated a printing company renowned for the high quality of its work. A collector himself, he encouraged her interest which had been aroused by the color and lucidity which make glass such a delight to behold. She began to study the subject of glass-making and attended seminars at the Corning Museum of Glass. She decided to specialize in Sandwich glass and became a regular visitor to shops and auctions in Massachusetts and later New Hampshire when she and Albert moved to Temple. There, the house accommodated not only the glass but an extraordinary collection of tools and household devices. One of her major accomplishments was a collection of glass for the Byam House, which she and Albert donated to the Chelmsford Historical Society.

In 1974, Albert and Priscilla Murray gave The Murray Collection of Glass to The Currier Gallery of Art. In the concept of the gift and during the arrangements for the transfer, the Murrays were assisted by Roland and Marian Sallada who were also glass collectors. Not only did Albert and Priscilla make the collection available to the people of New Hampshire, they also provided funds for its management and for the publication of this catalogue.

The collection of glass at The Currier Gallery of Art represents primarily makers from New England who were active in the 19th century. For the first time The Murray Collection of Glass provided a comprehensive selection of examples of work by such renowned craftsmen and designers as Frederick Carder, Louis Comfort Tiffany, George and Thomas Woodall, and Emile Gallé, and from such glass houses as the Union Glass Company, Quezal, Durand, and Mount Washington. The collection encompasses the extraordinary range of colors and textures, forms, and techniques introduced by these late 19th and early 20th century makers of what has come to be called art glass. Moreover, in the years since the Murrays' gift, this collection has inspired others to give additional examples of art glass, thus maintaining the vitality of this important part of The Currier's collections.

This catalogue is the result of a strong collaborative effort. Albert and Priscilla Murray were an important part of the initial planning. Melvin E. Watts and curatorial interns Virginia Mathias and Lisa Yameen devoted many hours to compiling the catalogue text. Paul V. Gardner has given his time and expertise to write the introductory essay and assist Philip Zimmerman in editing the catalogue. Bill Finney directed his skills toward the photography, and Carl Zahn brought it all together. Roland and Marian Sallada have provided enthusiastic support and invaluable guidance in many ways.

This catalogue for The Murray Collection of Glass is a tribute to Sophie, Priscilla, and Albert Murray. Their gift has greatly enhanced the holdings of The Currier Gallery of Art. Every work of art needs both a creator and a spectator to fulfill its role and purpose. The Murray Collection of Glass shall never lack an appreciative audience.

ROBERT M. DOTY
Director
The Currier Gallery of Art

# ThE MURRAY COllECTiON of GLASS

The Murray Collection consists of nearly 400 pieces of fine European and American glass dating from about the 1870s to the 1920s. It includes many rare examples of Victorian, Art Nouveau, and Classical styles which are now generally called art glass. The Murrays began assembling their collection in the late 1940s and continued into the early 1970s. The fine pieces on view in The Currier Gallery of Art and published in this catalogue are a tribute to their enthusiasm and discrimination.

## CAMEO GLASS

Some of the rarest pieces in the collection are English Cameo glass. These exquisite glass creations were produced in the last decades of the 19th century when English glassmakers revived this ancient decorative technique. Although cameo glass pieces are recorded as having been made as early as the Hellenistic Era, it was the Roman glassmakers who brought this luxury glass to a high degree of excellence in the early years of the Empire. This costly technique was seldom employed in the later Roman Empire and seems to have died out completely in Europe after the 5th century. A few Islamic artisans used it in the 10th century, and the Chinese produced some cameo glass in the 18th and 19th centuries. The English revival began in the 1870s when John Northwood I copied in glass the world famous Portland Vase, a masterpiece made by Roman artisans in the late 1st century B.C. or early 1st century A.D. Northwood's pupils and contemporaries, including George and Thomas Woodall, Frederick Carder, Alphonse Lecheveral, Joseph Locke, and John Northwood II, brought the art of cameo glass to an almost unbelievable peak of perfection during the 1880s and 1890s.

George Woodall is now considered the most skillful of these English cameo glass artists. He and the "Woodall Team," comprised of his brother Thomas and four other cameo glass artists, are responsible for some of the finest English cameo glass in the Murray Collection, including the important sapphire blue 18-inch high vase decorated with beautifully carved hollyhock and apple blossoms, a handsome framed plaque with central motif of "Cupid on a Lioness," and a classical vase having a full length figure of "Pandora" (Figs. 1, 2, and 3). Another fine example is a small jar and cover bearing an exquisitely carved depiction of "Zeus and Ganymede" and a regal miniature portrait of "Queen Victoria" mounted in a hinged metal stand (Figs. 4 and 5). Three vases, one in citron yellow with a white parrot-tulip design and a pair in orange with white apple blossom sprays and white linings, round out the English cameo glass in the collection (Figs. 6 and 7).

The development of cameo glass on the Continent paralleled its popularity in England. Famous glassmakers such as Emile Gallé (Fig. 8) and Daum Frères (Figs. 9 and 10) specialized in Art Nouveau cameo glass and along with Cristallerie Schneider, marked "Le Verre Francais," are represented by glass vases in this style (Fig. 11).

## LATE 19TH CENTURY
### Continental European and English Styles and Techniques

In contrast to Gallé's Art Nouveau fantasies, this delightfully diversified collection also includes design styles ranging from the perennially favorite Classical forms to Victorian extravagances. Notable among these are a pair of Classical vases on circular pedestals reminiscent of 18th century Sèvres porcelain (Fig. 12), and an elegant covered punch bowl with nine matching cups having alternating gold and silver background panels decorated with sprays of pink and yellow roses painted in enamel colors (Fig. 13).

The Victorian love of ornamentation is exemplified by frilled glass baskets with applied fruit, flowers, and twisted thorn handles (Fig. 14), along with a pair of white glass lustres with pink linings, ruffled tops, and cut crystal pendants (Fig. 15), which may have graced the mantelpiece of a 19th century parlor. Other Victorian delights are two ruby and crystal glass epergnes complete with trumpet-shaped vases and small sweetmeat baskets hanging from spiraled glass arms (Fig. 16).

One of the most popular types of art glass in 19th century Europe and America was "Satin Glass," also called "Pearl Satin Ware" and "Pearl Ware." As the name implies, this glass has a soft lustrous surface texture, resembling satin, and usually produced by an acid dip. Satin Glass shapes were often a blend of Classical and Victorian forms combined with "air-trap" designs (Fig. 17). Air-trap patterns are made by enclosing air bubbles in controlled shapes and designs between two or more layers of transparent or translucent glass. When air-trap patterns are included, the ware was sometimes called "Mother-of-Pearl" satin glass and given descriptive names like "diamond-quilted," "drape," "swirl," and "raindrop" which are some of the notable air-trap designs in the collection (Fig. 18).

Other innovative 19th century decorative techniques include vases and bowls with "marbleized" (Fig. 19), "spangled" (Fig. 20), "coralene" (Fig. 21), "silver overlay" (Fig. 22), and "millefiori" (Fig. 23) decorations made in Continental Europe, England, and America.

## CUT AND ENGRAVED CRYSTAL GLASS
## 19th and 20th Century

Ever since George Ravenscroft perfected his lead glass formula in London about 1676, lead crystal glass has been an important part of glass production, first in England, then in Ireland and Continental Europe, and later in America. The addition of lead oxide to the glass formula (up to about 33% in the best types) produces a glass of greater brilliance and resonance than non-lead glass. Decorative lead crystal glass and tablewares in the collection include a tiered centerpiece (Fig. 24), compotes (Figs. 25 and 26), and decanters (Fig. 27) expertly cut in traditional Anglo-Irish styles.

Engraved decorations combined with cut motifs give elegance and beauty to two English 19th century vases. One has an overall design featuring birds and floral sprays (Fig. 28). The other, signed "Geo Woodall", has a figure of "Undine" engraved in an oval reserve surrounded by cut borders and foliate motifs (Fig. 29).

Notable among the other decorative tablewares is a handsome centerbowl (Fig. 30) with patterns cut and engraved through a ruby stain on the outer surface of the crystal glass in Bohemian style. A delightful Art Nouveau syrup jug (Fig. 31) engraved with iris blooms and leaves has repoussé sterling silver mounts and is marked "Hawkes."

## AMERICAN ART GLASS

American glassmakers of the late 19th and early 20th century, while still somewhat influenced by European trends, were actively engaged in producing new colors and making technical advances. These developments allowed them to compete with European imports and to stimulate sales of American glassware at home and abroad. Examples of these techniques comprise about two-thirds of the Murray Collection.

In the 1870s the Victorian taste was still in vogue, and glassmakers in New England and the Pittsburgh, Pennsylvania, and Wheeling, West Virginia, areas vied with each other and challenged their European competitors with a variety of new techniques and colors to meet this demand. One of the most popular of the new colors they developed was the New England Glass Company's Amberina, a transparent glass shading from amber at the base to a rich ruby

10

red at the top. This shading was accomplished "at the fire" by cooling the upper portion of the glass object with compressed air and then reheating the cooled portion. This caused the ruby color to develop — a process called "striking" by the glassmakers (Fig. 32). Amberina was patented by the New England Glass Company in 1883 and sold so well that the nearby Mount Washington Glass Company lost no time in producing a glass so similar that the company narrowly avoided a lawsuit by hastily patenting their glass under the name of "Rose Amber." Types of Amberina were also made by the Libbey Glass Company, Toledo, Ohio; Hobbs, Brockunier & Company, Wheeling, West Virginia; and in England.

Other popular types of art glass made by the New England Glass Company and represented in the collection are Agata, Pomona (Fig. 33), and the extremely rare Plated Amberina (Fig. 34). Another rare glass, Opaque Green (Fig. 35), is actually a slightly translucent light green with a matte finish and a mottled metallic stain border around the top. The decorative staining is very similar to the metallic ornament found on Agata.

The continued success of shaded glasses influenced Mount Washington to produce "Burmese," a translucent glass shading from a delicate yellow base to a soft rose top, which they patented in 1886 (Fig. 36). The pastel shadings of this glass appealed to the American trade at the time and is avidly sought by collectors today. When Burmese glass was exhibited in England, it so caught the fancy of Queen Victoria that Thomas Webb & Sons of the Stourbridge area obtained a license to produce it in England under the name "Queen's Burmese" (Fig. 37).

Queen's Burmese was especially adaptable to fairy lamps. These were popular lighting adjuncts to Victorian bedrooms and garden parties, where they were often used by the dozens to give candlelight an even more romantic glow. The Murray Collection has excellent examples of these "Clarke's Patented Pyramid Night Lights," including a very rare triple fairy lamp and bud vase centerpiece (Fig. 38). Burmese-type glass has been made in the 20th century in Continental Europe and by the Gundersen-Pairpoint Glass Works (successors to Mount Washington) in the 1950s.

The sale of Mary Morgan's Chinese porcelain Peach Bloom vase in 1886 for an unbelievable $18,000.00 (due to a clerk's error in misreading the $1,800.00 price) sparked an immediate response from contemporary glassmakers. Before the year ended, three American factories had "Peach Blow" type glass on the market. They were the New England Glass Company and the Mount Washington Glass Company in Massachusetts, and the Hobbs, Brockunier & Company in Wheeling, West Virginia. Mount Washington was the first to file trade-name papers, thereby insuring their exclusive use of the name "Peach Blow." Their translucent glass shaded from bluish white at the base to a rose top. The New England Glass Company used the name "Wild Rose" for a somewhat similar shaded glass (Fig. 39). Hobbs, Brockunier & Company produced "Coral," a much stronger color, which shaded from yellow to ruby red and was cased over a white lining, which further intensified the color. Among the most popular and decorative pieces of "Coral," or "Wheeling Peachblow" as it is now usually called, were the now-rare vases made in approximately the same size and shape as the Morgan "Peach Bloom" porcelain vase. These could also be bought with molded amber glass stands formed by five dragon-like beasts (Fig. 40). Peach Blow glass was made about the same time by English and Bohemian firms. Between 1952 and 1957, the Gundersen-Pairpoint Glass Works revived the color in what is now called "Gundersen-Pairpoint Peach Blow" (Fig. 41).

Burmese, Peach Blow, and the purloined Rose Amber all depended on shaded colorings for their popularity. In contrast to these, Royal Flemish (Fig. 42) and Crown Milano (Fig. 43), made by the Mount Washington Glass Company in the 1890s, relied on gilded and enameled decorations for their appeal to the Victorian taste. These elaborately decorated pieces were of translucent glass stained and painted in designs ranging from pseudo-Roman coins on a background suggesting stained glass to elegantly jeweled and gilded floral motifs.

Another rarity, now called "Mount Washington Cameo," shows the influence of English cameo designs. These pieces are often in opaque white with a thin pink casing which has an acid-etched design including a female head in profile surrounded by foliate decorations (Fig. 44).

Less well-known than the New England Glass Company and Mount Washington productions, but of interest to collectors of late 19th century American art glass, are the decorative "Wave Crest" covered jars made by C. F. Monroe of Meriden, Connecticut, made about 1898, and the earlier wares of Smith Brothers of New Bedford, Massachusetts, done in the 1870s (Fig. 45).

As the turn of the century approached, other American glassmakers besides those already mentioned began to produce art glass in Art Nouveau and other styles. The Murrays took a special interest in these productions and the collection is rich in carefully selected rarities from a number of these factories. Among these, the Union Glass Company, Somerville, Massachusetts (1854-1924), was one of the few 19th century glass factories which survived well into the 20th. Although its productions were of such high calibre that the Smithsonian Institution accepted a collection of its glass in 1905, this important factory has not received the recognition it deserves from historians and collectors. During the seventy years it was in operation, its productions ranged from Venetian and Bohemian styles (Fig. 46) to iridescent tablewares and vases (Fig. 47). The 17 pieces in the Murray Collection

give viewers an unusual opportunity to study the style and quality of some of the Union Glass Company's 20th century glass.

Among the American factories represented in the collection which are perhaps better known than the Union Glass Company are Quezal Art Glass & Decorating Company, Brooklyn, New York; Durand Art Glass Company, Vineland, New Jersey (Fig. 48); and the Imperial Glass Company, Bellaire, Ohio. However, the major portion of the American 20th century glass in the Murray Collection was produced in the first decades of the 20th century by the two giants of American early 20th century glassmaking, Louis Comfort Tiffany and Frederick Carder of Steuben Glass Works.

Louis Comfort Tiffany was the first American artist in glass to follow the European trends and produce Art Nouveau glass at his Stourbridge Glass Company (renamed Tiffany Furnaces in 1902) in Corona, Long Island, New York, in 1893. Floriform vases were some of his most successful Art Nouveau forms and are splendidly represented in the collection. These creations are in gold and blue iridescent shadings, sometimes with applied feathers, leaves, and trailed tendrils (Fig. 50). Tiffany called these and all his other art glass pieces "Favrile" glass, a name probably derived from "fabrile" meaning "hand made," which he registered in the U.S. Patent Office in 1894. Other fine examples of Tiffany's Favrile include such rarities as a glowing ruby-red vase with green leaves and vines enclosed between thin glass layers with opalescent shadings (Fig. 51); a vase with morning glories enclosed in heavy crystal glass (Fig. 52); and an exquisite and extremely rare carved cameo Agate glass vase with fish decorations in Chinese style (Fig. 53). Finally, a carefully executed Cypriote vase suggests the imperfections, rough workmanship, and effects of age associated with ancient glass (Fig. 54).

Frederick Carder, a contemporary and competitor of Tiffany, had designed art glass for Stevens & Williams in Brierley Hill, Staffordshire, England, in the 1880s and 1890s. After he moved to Corning, New York, in 1903, where he founded the Steuben Glass Works, he continued to make art glass in a wide variety of styles for the next three decades.

Carder Steuben rarities in the collection feature vases and decorative tablewares in Gold and Blue Aurene, which was Carder's answer to Tiffany's iridescent Favrile (Fig. 55). A rare Brown Aurene shade gives a rich character to a brass desk lamp especially suitable for a library or office (Fig. 56). In contrast to the somber and formal Brown Aurene, a lustrous Ivrene vase having a center trumpet flanked by calla lilies asserts Carder's continuing love of Art Nouveau even in the 1920s (Fig. 57). European and Oriental influences are apparent in a handsome Alabaster vase cased with Jade Green and a pair of candlesticks double-etched in the "Dragon" pattern (Fig. 58). Among Steuben's elegant dressing table accessories are a Calcite boudoir lamp with applied green and Gold Aurene feather decorations (Fig. 47), and a massive cut crystal cologne bottle having a Cintra center surrounded by controlled bubbles (Fig. 59). The use of bubbles as a key element of design is also evident in a rare lamp base of Cluthra glass acid-etched in the "Chang" pattern with frosted colorless glass handles applied in three layers (Fig. 60). Other colorful decorative pieces in sparkling yellows, blues, and greens (Fig. 61) — many showing Venetian influences — and a free-style "Grotesque" bowl (Fig. 62), along with many other objects in the collection, demonstrate the diversity of colors and hand-blowing manipulations of Steuben gaffers under Carder's masterful guidance.

The wide variety of glassmakers and decorative styles represented in the Murray Collection provide the viewer, collector, and student of Art Glass with an unusually rich source of information and enjoyment. The information in this cata-logue is, of necessity, limited in most instances to only the basic facts, and it is hoped those who wish to learn more about the areas represented will consult the publications noted in the selected bibliography.

Selected Bibliography

Paul V. Gardner. *The Glass of Frederick Carder.* New York: Crown Publishers, 1971.

Sidney M. Goldstein, Leonard S. Rakow, and Juliette K. Rakow. *Cameo Glass: Masterpieces from 2000 Years of Glassblowing.* Corning, NY: Corning Museum of Glass, 1982.

Ray and Lee Grover. *Art Glass Nouveau.* Rutland, VT: Charles E. Tuttle Company, 1967.

Ray and Lee Grover. *English Cameo Glass.* New York: Crown Publishers, 1980.

Lowell Innes. *Pittsburgh Glass, 1797-1891.* Boston: Houghton Mifflin Company, 1976.

Robert Koch. *Louis C. Tiffany, Rebel in Glass.* New York: Crown Publishers, 1964.

Robert Koch. *Louis C. Tiffany's Glass - Bronzes - Lamps.* New York: Crown Publishers, 1971.

Hugh F. McKean. *The "Lost" Treasures of Louis Comfort Tiffany.* Garden City, NY: Doubleday & Company, 1980.

George S. and Helen McKearin. *200 Years of American Blown Glass.* Garden City, NY: Doubleday & Company, 1950.

George S. and Helen McKearin. *American Glass.* New York: Crown Publishers, 1941.

Albert Christian Revi. *Nineteenth Century Glass: Its Genesis and Development.* New York: Thomas Nelson & Sons, 1959.

Albert Christian Revi. *American Art Nouveau Glass.* New York: Thomas Nelson & Sons, 1968.

Kenneth M. Wilson. *New England Glass & Glassmaking.* New York: Thomas Y. Crowell Company, 1972.

# PLATES

Fig. 1. *Cameo Glass Vase,* c. 1885. Hollyhocks and apple
blossom sprays interspersed with garden insects carved in
coral red cased over white on a blue ground. Arabesque
border around neck and anthemion circlet on base. Attributed to the Woodall team, Thomas Webb & Sons, Stourbridge, England. (Ht.: 18 in., cat. no 6)

Fig. 2. *Cameo Glass Plaque*, late 19th century. Cupid riding
a lioness carved in white cased over an orange ground and
surrounded by a circle of floral sprays. Mounted in a gilded
wooden frame with cameo glass spandrels. Attributed to
George Woodall, Thomas Webb & Sons, Stourbridge,
England. (Ht.: 19¾ in., cat. no. 3)

Fig. 3. *Cameo Glass Vase*, 1889. Pandora holding the still unopened box. Carved in white cased over a dark topaz ground. ''Paris Exhibition 1889 / G. Woodall'' engraved in the gold-plated metal base with round ''gem cameo'' mark in bottom of vase. Thomas Webb & Sons, Stourbridge, England. (Ht.: 8½ in., cat. no. 4)

Fig. 4. *Cameo Glass Jar*, late 19th century. Zeus as an eagle bearing Ganymede through the clouds to become cupbearer to the Gods. Carved in white cased over a dark green (appearing black) ground. "Gem Cameo" mark of Thomas Webb & Sons impressed in bottom. Stourbridge, England. (Ht.: 6½ in., cat. no. 7)

Fig. 5. *Cameo Glass Portrait Plaque*, late 19th century.
Queen Victoria in formal regalia and wearing a Maltese
crown. Carved in white on a red background, and mounted
in a gilded metal frame. Probably done in celebration of her
diamond jubilee of 1897. Probably by George Woodall of
Thomas Webb & Sons, Stourbridge, England. (Ht.: 6½ in.,
cat. no. 2)

Fig. 6. *Cameo Glass Vase*, late 19th century. Parrot tulips
carved in white cased over a yellow-green ground. English.
(Ht.: 10⅛ in., cat. no. 5)

Fig. 7. *Pair of Cameo Glass Vases*, late 19th century. Dogwood blossoms carved in white cased over an orange-yellow ground with white linings. English. (Ht.: 7¼ in., cat.
no. 1)

Fig. 8. *Cameo Glass Vases*, late 19th to early 20th century.
Made by Emile Gallé and his glass works which continued
to operate for eight years after his death in 1905. Glass
made after 1905 includes a star after the Gallé name.
Nancy, France. (Ht. of vase on left: 12¼ in., cat. nos. 14,
19, 15, 13, 16, 17)

Fig. 9. *Diamond-shaped Vase*, late 19th to early 20th century. Crystal glass lined with transparent sapphire blue. Miniature landscapes etched in cameo style accented with painted black enamels. Gilded rim. Signed "Daum/Nancy" with Cross of Lorraine. Daum Frères (Cristalleries de Nancy), Nancy, France. (Ht.: 7⅛, cat. no. 9)

Fig. 10. *Vase*, late 19th to early 20th century. Acid-etched floral design in mottled red, yellow, and green glass cased over pale green glass with brown mottling at base. Signed ''Daum/Nancy'' with Cross of Lorraine. Cristalleries de Nancy, Nancy, France. (Ht.: 5½ in., cat. no. 8)

Fig. 11. *Vase*, late 19th century. Acid-etched fruit pattern in speckled red and green cased over layers of colorless and mottled red and green glass. Marked "Le Verre Francais," a signature used by Cristallerie Schneider, France. (Ht.: 5⅛ in., cat. no. 11)

Fig. 12. *Pair of Vases*, mid 19th century. Classically-styled opalescent glass with enameled pastoral scenes in white reserves on a dark green ground, reminiscent of Sèvres porcelain. Bases are enameled in brown with gilded accents. Probably Bohemian. (Ht.: 12¼ in., cat. no. 68)

Fig. 13. *Covered Punch Bowl with Ladle and Glasses,*
1850-1900. Ruby-stained colorless glass with enameled floral sprays on alternate gold and silver vertical-striped
panels. European, possibly Bohemian. (Ht.: 14¾ in., cat.
no. 75)

Fig. 14. *Baskets*, late 19th century. Decorated "at the fire" with applied flowers and handles. Tooled handles, like that on the right, are often called "twisted thorn" handles. The basket on the left may be Austrian, the others are probably English. (Ht. of basket on left: 6½ in., cat. nos. 49, 52, 47)

Fig. 15. *Pair of Lustres*, late 19th century. Opaque white glass cased over pink and decorated with polychrome enameled floral sprays and cut crystal pendants. Probably English. (Ht.: 14¾, cat. no. 45)

Fig. 16. *Epergne*, late 19th century. Transparent pink glass
shaded to colorless in trumpet shapes and baskets having
applied pale green tooled decorations. Probably English.
(Ht.: 19¼, cat. no. 40)

Fig. 17. *Satin Glass Bowl, Lamp, and Vase,* late 19th century. All made of shaded raspberry-colored glass with white linings in air-trap patterns of moiré (bowl), swirled, and ringed. The European lamp and shade may not have been together originally. The bowl and vase are probably English. (Ht. of lamp: 12¾, cat. nos. 26, 32, 36)

Fig. 18. *Satin Glass Ewer, Vases, and Berry Bowl*, late 19th
century. Left to right: rainbow striped in diamond-quilted
air-trap pattern, yellow in draped air-trap pattern, blue in
rain-drop air-trap pattern, and pink in diamond-quilted air-
trap pattern with enamel decoration. All probably English.
(Ht. of ewer: 7½, cat. nos. 30, 34, 37, 22)

Fig. 19. *Covered Butter Dish and Pitcher,* late 19th to early 20th century. Yellow-tinted glass with splotches of oxblood and white. Marbleized pitcher is in an inverted thumbprint pattern. Probably European. (Ht. of pitcher: 8⅜ in., cat. nos. 77, 78)

Fig. 20. *Spangled Vase and Rose Bowl*, late 19th century.
Made of a layer of glass rolled in metallic flakes, the apri-
cot-colored vase on the left has silver flecks, white lining,
and colorless thorn handles. The rose bowl is transparent
pink with white and silver flecks. Both probably Hobbs,
Brockunier & Company, Wheeling, WV. (Ht. of vase: 7¼
in., cat. nos. 339, 340)

Fig. 21. *Coralene Vases*, 1880-1900. A variety of satin glass decorated with tiny glass beads fused to the surface, usually in coral-like formations. Probably Mount Washington Glass Company, New Bedford, MA, although made elsewhere in the United States and Europe. (Ht. of vase on left: 9 in., cat. nos. 120, 118, 117, 119)

Fig. 22. *Silver Overlay Vases*, late 19th to early 20th century. Gold iridescent glass with designs in silver by Quezal Art Glass and Decorating Company, Brooklyn, NY (left), and Loetz of Austria (right). (Ht. of vase on left: 9 in., cat. nos. 318, 65)

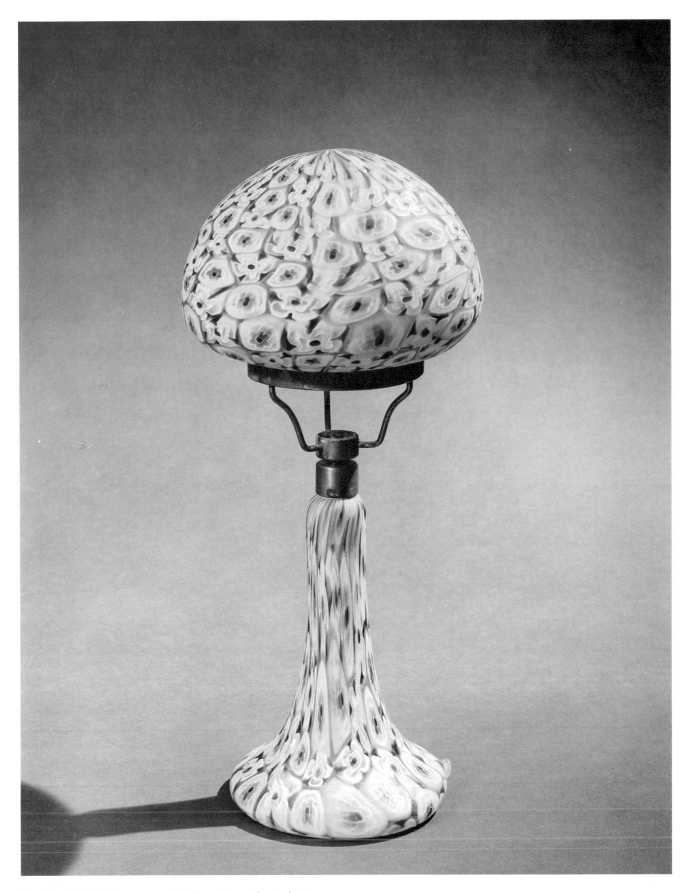

Fig. 23. *Millefiori Lamp*, early 20th century. The technique
used in this lamp, in which sections of colored glass rods
are fused together in a mosaic pattern, originated in ancient
times. It was revived by Venetian glassmakers in the mid
16th century and has been produced there and elsewhere
since. Venice, Italy. (Ht.: 13 in., cat. no. 66)

Fig. 24. *Tiered Epergne Centerpiece*, 19th century. Made of lead crystal glass and cut in strawberry diamond pattern in an Anglo-Irish style. Probably English. (Ht.: 16½ in., cat. no. 368)

Fig. 25. *Covered Compote*, 19th century. Lead crystal glass
cut in thumbprint pattern. Note air bubbles in stem and
finial. Probably Anglo-Irish. (Ht.: 12¾ in., cat. no. 365)

Fig. 26. *Compote*, late 19th century. Lead crystal glass cut
with panel flutings and petal scalloped rim. Probably
English. (Ht.: 9¼ in., cat. no. 364)

Fig. 27. *Ewer and Decanter*, late 19th century. Lead crystal glass cut in diamond and fan pattern with a ''D'' monogram in Old English style in cartouche. England or United States (Pittsburgh or Corning). (Ht. of ewer: 10¼ in., cat. nos. 366, 367)

Fig. 28. *Vase*, late 19th century. Lead crystal glass wheel-engraved with birds and floral sprays. Gilded rims and panel-cut stem with gold filigree designs. Attributed to Stevens & Williams, Brierley Hill, England. (Ht.: 10½ in., cat. no. 351)

Fig. 29. *Vase*, late 19th century. Lead crystal glass with
engraved figure of Undine, a fabled water spirit, set within
an oval medallion surrounded by cut and engraved decorations. Signed "Geo Woodall" in script within the oval and
stamped with the ribbon mark of Thomas Webb & Sons on
bottom. Stourbridge, England. (Ht.: 13 in., cat. no. 352)

Fig. 30. *Bowl*, 19th century. Floral border and strawberry diamond pattern engraved and cut through outside ruby stain to crystal glass matrix. Probably Bohemian. (Dia.: 11 in., cat. no. 370)

Fig. 31. *Syrup Jug*, late 19th to early 20th century. Crystal glass cut and engraved with iris blooms and leaves in an Art Nouveau style with silver repoussé mounts. Marked "Hawkes" for T.G. Hawkes & Company, Corning, NY. (Ht.: 6¾ in., cat. no. 356)

Fig. 32. *Amberina Pitcher and Glasses*, 1880s. Developed and patented by the New England Glass Works in 1883, this transparent glass typically shades from an amber base to a ruby top. The pitcher is unusual as it reverses this coloring. Amberina was quickly copied by other factories. These pieces were probably made by the New England Glass Company, East Cambridge, MA. (Ht. of pitcher: 7¾, cat. nos. 170, 168, 169, 177, 179, 165)

Fig. 33. *Pomona Glass Group*, 1885-1888. Delicate shadings of amber and blue stain accent this acid-etched glass patented in 1885 and 1886 by Joseph Locke of the New England Glass Company, East Cambridge, MA. (Ht. of pitcher: 7 in., cat. nos. 158, 153, 160, 152, 154)

Fig. 34. *Plated Amberina Syrup Pitcher and Plate*, 1883-1888. Made by the New England Glass Company, East Cambridge, MA, with silver-plated mounts and plate marked by James W. Tufts of Boston. (Ht.: 5⅞ in., cat. no. 161)

Fig. 35. *"Opaque Green" Cup*, c. 1887. This rare kind of glass is actually a slightly translucent green glass with mottled metallic staining, a decorative technique also used in Agata glass. Attributed to the New England Glass Company, East Cambridge, MA. (Ht.: 3¼ in., cat. no. 192)

Fig. 36. *Burmese Vase and Toothpick Holder*, 1952-1957 and 1883-1894. Patented by the Mount Washington Glass Company in 1885, Burmese glass was usually made in matte finish, unlike these rare examples in bright or glossy finish. Burmese glass was revived in the 1950s by the Gun- dersen-Pairpoint Glass Works, maker of the vase and suc- cessor to the Mount Washington Glass Company, maker of the toothpick holder. (Ht. of vase: 7⅜ in., cat. nos. 116, 93)

Fig. 37. *Queen's Burmese Vases and Gemel Bottle*, late
19th century. Made by and vases marked by Thomas Webb
& Sons, Stourbridge, England. (Ht. of vase on left: 7¾ in.,
cat. nos. 104, 95, 102)

Fig. 38. *Queen's Burmese Triple Fairy Lamp and Bud Vase Centerpiece*, late 19th century. Marked "S. Clark Patent Trade Mark Fairy" on the pressed colorless glass bases and liners. English. (Ht.: 9 in., cat. no. 97)

Fig. 39. *Wild Rose Tumbler, Bowl, and Vase,* 1886-1888.
Now called by the generic term peach blow glass, these
pieces by the New England Glass Company, East Cambridge, MA, were marketed as ''Wild Rose.'' (Ht. of vase:
8½ in., cat. nos. 127, 126, 128)

Fig. 40. *One of a Pair of "Morgan" Vases*, c. 1886. Similar
in shape to the Morgan Chinese Peach Bloom porcelain
vase, this vase is an important example of Wheeling Peach
Blow, made and sold by the Hobbs, Brockunier & Company, Wheeling, WV, as "Coral Glass." (Ht.: 10 in., cat.
no. 139)

Fig. 41. *Peach Blow Cup and Saucer, Candlestick, and Saucer with handle*, 1952-1957. Gundersen-Pairpoint Glass Works, New Bedford, MA. (Ht. of candlestick: 7¾ in., cat. nos. 145, 143, 148)

Fig. 42. *Royal Flemish Biscuit or Cookie Jars*, 1890s. Fine examples of these rare pieces. Mount Washington Glass Company, New Bedford, MA. (Ht. of jar on right: 8¼ in., cat. nos. 194, 196)

Fig. 43. *Royal Flemish and Crown Milano Cookie Jars and Vase*, 1890s. Mount Washington Glass Company, New Bedford, MA, and others. (Ht. of jar on left: 7½ in., cat. nos. 195, 69, 200)

Fig. 45. *Opal Glass Covered Boxes, Jar, and Bowl*, late 19th century. Molded and decorated with painted and raised enameling. The boxes are marked "Wave Crest" and were made by C.F. Monroe Company, Meriden, CT. The jar was made by Smith Brothers, New Bedford, MA. (Ht. of large jar: 5¼ in., cat. nos. 335, 337, 336, 338, 334)

Fig. 44. *Bride's Basket or Berry Bowl and Vase*, late 19th
century. Acid-etched design in pink cased over white,
called "Mount Washington Cameo." Mount Washington
Glass Company, New Bedford, MA. (Ht. of vase: 10½ in.,
cat. nos. 201, 203)

Fig. 46. *Lamp*, early 20th century. Crystal glass with medallions, fans, thumbprint, and other decorations cut through ruby layer. Probably Union Glass Company, Somerville, MA. (Ht.: 15 in., cat. no. 314)

Fig. 47. *Feather Pull-up Vases and Lamp*, 1900-1925. Competing companies used similar colors and decorative techniques. Two vases on left were made by the Union Glass Company, Somerville, MA; the next vase was made by Quezal Art Glass and Decorating Company, Brooklyn, NY; and the lamp was made by Steuben Glass Works, Corning, NY. (Ht. of lamp: 12 in., cat. nos. 299, 298, 315, 220)

Fig. 48. *Feather Pull-up Vase*, 1924-1933. Translucent blue decoration on crystal glass with cobalt blue top. Made and marked by Durand Art Glass Company, Vineland, NJ, under the direction of Emil Larsen. (Ht.: 8½ in., cat. no. 319)

Fig. 49. *Iridescent Vase*, early 20th century. Heavy green
iridescent mottled swags on cream base with reddish-orange
iridescent lining and three looped feet. Possibly Loetz, Austria. (Ht.: 6¼ in., cat. no. 63)

Fig. 50. *Tiffany Favrile Vases*, 1893-1920. A representative group of the hand-blown decorative glass made at the Tiffany Furnaces in Corona, Long Island, NY. The name ''Favrile'' (hand wrought) was applied to a wide variety of pieces regardless of form, color, or technique since 1894 when it was registered with the U.S. Patent Office. (Ht. of tallest vase: 16 in., cat. nos. 283, 286, 284, 280, 259, 258, 270, 287, 257, 285)

Fig. 51. *Vase*, 1910s. Ruby glass with shaded opal casing decorated with applied yellow, brown, and green foliage. Marked "9452 H L. C. Tiffany - Favrile." Tiffany Furnaces, Corona, NY. (Ht.: 7¾ in., cat. no. 293)

Fig. 52. *Morning Glory Vase*, 1910s. Green tinted transparent body with morning glory blossoms surrounded by leaves and tendrils imbedded in the upper portion. Marked "8060 L L. C. Tiffany Favrile." Tiffany Furnaces, Corona, NY. (Ht.: 6¼ in., cat. no. 294)

Fig. 53. *Octagonal Vase*, 1900-1920. Very rare cameo-carved Chinese dragon design in white cased over yellow-green Agate glass. Marked "103A Coll. L. C. Tiffany Favrile." Tiffany Furnaces, Corona, NY. (Ht.: 3¾ in., cat. no. 256)

Fig. 54. *Cypriote Vase*, early 20th century. Cloudy-white and irregularly pitted translucent yellow glass with light purple shading at base. Marked "844 T L. C. Tiffany - Favrile." Tiffany Furnaces, Corona, NY. (Ht.: 4¼ in., cat. no. 262)

Fig. 55. *Blue Aurene Group*, 1920-1930. All are marked "Aurene" except the whimsical stocking darner, which was probably made after hours by a gaffer to take home. Steuben Division of Corning Glass Works, Corning, NY. (Ht. of "rustic" bud vase: 6⅜ in., cat. nos. 231, 232, 234, 235)

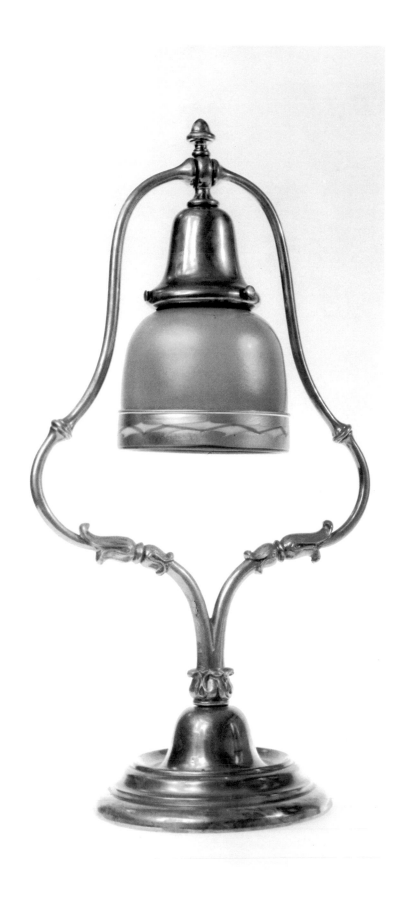

Fig. 56. *Brown Aurene Lamp,* c. 1915. Bronze lamp with
shade of brown-colored iridescent layer of glass cased over
translucent white with characteristic criss-crossed brown and
white threading "rubbed into" the Gold Aurene border.
Steuben mark stamped in silver. Steuben Glass Works,
Corning, NY. (Ht.: 16½ in., cat. no. 245)

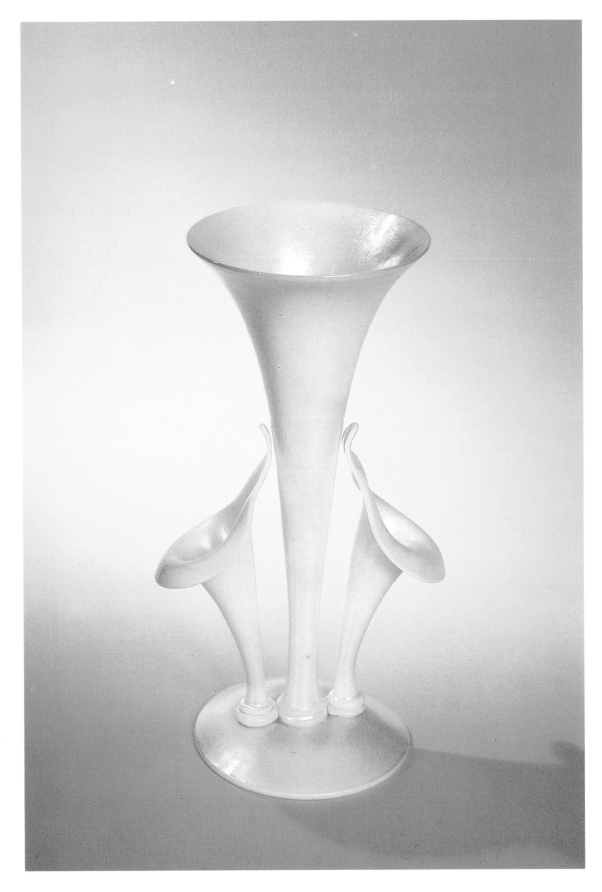

Fig. 57. *Trumpet Vase with Calla Lilies*, 1920-1930. Ivrene
glass. Steuben Division of Corning Glass Works, Corning,
NY. (Ht.: 12 in., cat. no. 252)

Fig. 58. *Vase and Pair of Candlesticks*, 1920-1930. Alabaster glass cased with Jade Green and acid-etched in "Dragon" pattern (vase) and "Chinese" pattern (candlesticks). Steuben Division of Corning Glass Works, Corning, NY. (Ht. of vase: 9½ in., cat. nos. 206, 205)

Fig. 59. *Cintra Cologne Bottle*, late 1920s. Cintra center, a powdered glass, shading from black to white and cased in heavy crystal glass with controlled bubbles and cut decorations. Acid-stamped with fleur-de-lis mark of Steuben Division of Corning Glass Works, Corning, NY. (Ht.: 8½ in., cat. no. 218)

Fig. 60. *Cluthra Lamp Base,* 1920-1930. Pink Cluthra glass cased in Pomona Green and acid-etched in "Chang" pattern. Also made to be a vase, this particular example is drilled through the bottom for use as a lamp. Steuben Division of Corning Glass Works, Corning, NY. (Ht.: 12¾ in., cat. no. 219)

Fig. 61. *Steuben Glass Group*, 1920-1930. Bowl in light
Topaz with Pomona Green foot, vase in Bristol Yellow, and
plate in Celeste Blue. Steuben Division of Corning Glass
Works, Corning, NY. (Ht. of vase: 6⅝ in., cat. nos. 209,
215, 210)

Fig. 62. *"Grotesque" Bowl,* late 1920s to early 1930s. Termed "Grotesque" by Frederick Carder, these bowls were first blown in a ribbed mold, then flared and skillfully pulled into their final shape. Marked "Steuben" in acid-stamped script for the Steuben Division of Corning Glass Works, Corning, NY. (Ht.: 6 in., cat. no 217)

# CATALOGUE

## Notes to catalogue entries

Only the makers of marked objects are identified as such without qualification. "Attributed to" denotes with reasonable certainty the maker of an unmarked object. "Probably" and "possibly" reflect progressively greater uncertainty in establishing the identity of the maker. Identification of geographical origin follows the same general format.

All measurements are in inches. Height precedes length and width or diameter (identified as "dia").

Catalogue numbers conform to Currier Gallery accession numbers, which in their complete form include the numerical prefix "1974.33."

## CAMEO GLASS

**1**
PAIR OF VASES, late 19th century
Probably England
7¼ x 4⅝ (dia); dogwood blossoms carved in white cased over frosted orange-yellow ground with applied frosted colorless glass foot and white lining. (Fig. 7)

**2**
PORTRAIT PLAQUE, late 19th century
Attributed to Thomas Webb & Sons, probably George Woodall, Stourbridge, England
6½ x 5 (oval glass), 9⅜ x 8⅝ x 3½ (stand); Queen Victoria carved in white cased over frosted red ground, gilded metal stand. (Fig. 5)

**3**
PLAQUE, late 19th century
Attributed to George Woodall, Thomas Webb & Sons, Stourbridge, England
19¾ x 19½ x 1⅝; Cupid riding a lioness carved in white cased over frosted orange-yellow ground, mounted in a gilded and painted wood frame with cameo glass spandrels. (Fig. 2)

**4**
VASE, 1889
"Paris Exhibition 1889 / G. Woodall" engraved in foot, round "gem cameo" mark impressed in bottom
George Woodall, Thomas Webb & Sons, Stourbridge, England
8½ x 4 (dia); Pandora carved in white cased over frosted brown (dark topaz) ground, engraved gilded metal foot. (Fig. 3)

**5**
VASE, late 19th century
Probably England
10⅛ x 4 (dia); Parrot tulips carved in white cased over frosted yellow-green ground. (Fig. 6)

**6**
VASE, c. 1885
Attributed to the Woodall Team, Thomas Webb & Sons, Stourbridge, England
18 x 9 (dia); hollyhocks, apple blossoms, and insects carved in coral red cased over white over frosted blue ground. (Fig. 1)

**7**
COVERED JAR, late 19th century
Round "gem cameo" mark impressed in bottom
Thomas Webb & Sons, Stourbridge, England
6½ x 4 (dia); Zeus as an eagle bearing Ganymede carved in white cased over deep green (appearing black) ground. (Fig. 4, cover)

**8**
VASE, late 19th to early 20th century
"Daum / Nancy" with Cross of Lorraine etched in relief on side
Cristalleries de Nancy, Nancy, France
$5\frac{1}{2}$ x $5\frac{1}{4}$ (dia); acid-etched floral design in mottled red, yellow, and green cased over pale green glass with brown mottling at base. (Fig. 10)

**9**
DIAMOND-SHAPED VASE, late 19th to early 20th century
Cross of Lorraine and "Daum /Nancy" in gold on base
Daum Frères (Cristalleries de Nancy), Nancy, France
$7\frac{1}{8}$ x $3\frac{1}{4}$ x $2\frac{3}{4}$; landscapes acid-etched in colorless glass lined with transparent blue glass, accented with painted black enamel and gilded highlights and rim. (Fig. 9)

**10**
RECTANGULAR VASE, late 19th to early 20th century
Probably Europe
$7\frac{1}{4}$ x $3\frac{3}{8}$ x$2\frac{5}{8}$; acid-etched colorless glass lined with transparent amethyst glass, gilded highlights.

**11**
VASE, late 19th century
"Le Verre Francais" etched around base
Cristallerie Schneider, France
$5\frac{1}{8}$ x $6\frac{3}{4}$ (dia); fruit pattern acid-etched in speckled red and green cased over colorless over mottled red and green glass. (Fig. 11)

**12**
BOWL, late 19th century
"Le Verre Francais France" engraved on bottom
Cristallerie Schneider, France
$2\frac{1}{8}$ x 8 (dia); floral pattern acid-etched in dark blue cased over mottled orange over colorless over mottled yellow glass.

**13**
VASE, late 19th century
"Gallé" in relief on side
Emile Gallé, Nancy, France
13 x $6\frac{3}{4}$ x $4\frac{3}{8}$; iris blossom and leaves acid-etched in amethyst cased over transluscent colorless glass. (Fig. 8)

**14**
VASE, early 20th century, 1905-1913
"Gallé" with star in relief on side
Emile Gallé, Nancy, France
$12\frac{1}{4}$ x 4 (dia); floral pattern acid-etched in olive green cased over frosted yellow and colorless glass. (Fig. 8)

**15**
VASE, late 19th century
"Gallé" in relief on side
Emile Gallé, Nancy, France
$5\frac{3}{4}$ x $3\frac{3}{8}$ (dia); floral pattern acid-etched in green cased over yellow-green and orange over frosted colorless glass. (Fig. 8)

**16**
VASE, late 19th century
"Gallé" in relief on side
Emile Gallé, Nancy, France
$6\frac{1}{2}$ x $3\frac{1}{8}$ x $2\frac{1}{8}$; floral pattern acid-etched in amethyst cased over green over frosted colorless glass. (Fig. 8)

**17**
VASE, late 19th century
"Gallé" in relief on side
Emile Gallé, Nancy, France
$5\frac{7}{8}$ x 2 (dia); floral pattern acid-etched in amethyst cased over frosted orange and colorless glass. (Fig. 8)

**18**
VASE, late 19th century
"Gallé" in relief on side
Emile Gallé, Nancy, France
$5\frac{3}{4}$ x $2\frac{3}{8}$ (dia); floral pattern acid-etched in amethyst cased over frosted colorless glass.

**19**
VASE, 1905-1913
"Gallé" with star in relief on side
Emile Gallé, Nancy, France
$5\frac{1}{2}$ x $3\frac{1}{4}$ (dia); floral pattern acid-etched in grayish-green cased over violet over frosted colorless glass. (Fig. 8)

## SATIN GLASS

**20**
BOWL, late 19th century
Probably England
$1\frac{3}{8}$ x 6 (dia); diamond-quilted air-trap patterned peach satin glass cased over white with crimped rim and painted floral decoration.

**21**
BOWL, late 19th century
Probably England
$1\frac{3}{8}$ x 6 (dia); diamond-quilted air-trap patterned blue satin glass cased over white with crimped rim and painted floral decoration.

**22**
BERRY BOWL IN TWO-HANDLED STAND, late 19th century
Probably England
9 x 11 x 8 (bowl: $4\frac{3}{8}$ x $7\frac{7}{8}$ x $7\frac{7}{8}$); diamond-quilted air-trap patterned pink satin glass with white lining and painted floral decoration, crimped rim with colorless glass edge, and silver-plated stand marked "Rogers," Hartford, CT. (Fig. 18)

**23**
ROSE BOWL, late 19th to early 20th century
United States or Europe
$3\frac{3}{4}$ x $4\frac{1}{4}$ (dia); blue satin glass with white lining and ruffled top.

**24**
BOWL, late 19th to early 20th century
Attributed to Thomas Webb & Sons, Stourbridge, England
4 x $7\frac{1}{2}$ (dia); yellow satin glass shaded to dark yellow at crimped and scalloped top with white lining.

**25**
FOOTED ROSE BOWL, late 19th to early 20th century
United State or Europe
$6\frac{3}{4}$ x 5 (dia); pink shaded to white satin glass with scalloped top, white lining, and three applied colorless glass feet.

**26**
BOWL, late 19th century
Probably England
3¾ x 7¾ x 6¾; moiré air-trap patterned pink satin glass cased over white with folded rim, crimped and lined with colorless glass at edge. (Fig. 17)

**27**
PAIR OF EWERS, late 19th century
Probably Europe
8¾ x 4¼ x 3; melon-rib patterned pink satin glass with white lining, painted floral decoration with applied glass beads, and applied colorless glass handle.

**28**
EWER, late 19th century
Probably England
8¾ x 5¼ x 5; yellow shaded to white satin glass with white lining, scalloped top, and applied colorless glass tooled handle.

**29**
EWER, late 19th century
Probably England
8½ x 5⅝ x 4⅞; orange shaded to pink satin glass with white lining, scalloped top, and applied colorless glass tooled handle.

**30**
EWER, late 19th century
Probably England
7½ x 4⅜ x 4; diamond-quilted air-trap patterned rainbow-striped satin glass with white lining, crimped top, and applied colorless glass tooled handle. (Fig. 18)

**31**
POWDER BOX WITH COVER, late 19th century
Probably Europe
4½ x 4½ (dia); pink satin glass with white lining and painted floral decoration, silver-plated cover.

**32**
LAMP AND SHADE, late 19th century
Probably Europe
12¾ x 7¼ (dia); swirled air-trap patterned pink satin glass with white lining and applied colorless glass foot. (Fig. 17)

**33**
FAIRY LAMP, late 19th century
Probably England
4⅞ x 3⅞ (dia); yellow satin glass shaded to dark yellow at crimped top with pressed colorless "Clarke" base.

**34**
VASE, late 19th century
Probably England
4¾ x 4 x 3⅛; draped air-trap patterned yellow satin glass with white lining and applied colorless glass handles. (Fig. 18)

**35**
VASE, late 19th century
Possibly Stevens & Williams Ltd., Brierley Hill, England
11½ x 6¼ (dia); blue shaded to pink to white satin glass with white lining and gilded lip.

**36**
VASE, late 19th century
Probably England
7 x 5¼ (dia); ringed air-trap patterned pink satin glass with white lining. (Fig. 17)

**37**
VASE, late 19th century
United States or England
8¼ x 4¾ (dia); mold-blown blue satin glass in rain-drop air-trap pattern with white lining and scalloped top. (Fig. 18)

## MISCELLANEOUS ENGLISH GLASS

**38**
FOOTED BOWL, late 19th century
Probably England
4¾ x 8 (dia); transparent pink glass with three applied amber feet, applied amber and pink-and-white floral decorations, and scalloped top.

**39**
CRUET, late 19th century
Probably England
6 x 3½ x 3⅛; pattern-molded transparent pink glass with colorless glass handle and stopper.

**40**
EPERGNE, late 19th century
England
19¼ x 14 x 9½; transparent pink shaded to colorless glass in trumpet shapes with transparent pink to colorless baskets having applied colorless glass decoration, metal fittings. (Fig. 16)

**41**
EPERGNE, late 19th century
England
19 x 10½ (dia); swirled-rib patterned transparent pink and colorless glass in trumpet shapes, brass fittings.

**42**
PAIR OF FINGER BOWLS AND PLATES, late 19th century
Probably England
Bowl: 3 x 3¾ x 3¾, plate: 7½ (dia); transparent pink glass with silver-colored spangle "aventurine" decoration.

**43**
FINGERBOWL AND PLATE, late 19th to early 20th century
Probably England
Bowl: 2⅜ x 6⅛ (dia), plate: ⅞ x 6¾ (dia); transparent pink glass cased with colorless air-trap glass in diamond (bowl) and circle (plate) patterns with applied amber threads.

**44**
PAIR OF FINGERBOWLS AND PLATES, late 19th century
Probably England
Bowl: 3¼ x 5¾ (dia), plate: 2 x 8⅜ (dia); colorless glass with white looped glass in "Nailsea" style and applied red threads on ruffled rims of bowls and plates.

**45**
PAIR OF LUSTRES, late 19th century
Probably England
14¾ x 6⅜ (dia); opaque white cased over pink glass with polychrome enamel floral sprays and other decoration, cut colorless glass pendants. (Fig. 15)

## BASKETS

**46**
BASKET, late 19th century
Attributed to Thomas Webb & Sons, Stourbridge, England
5¼ x 4¾ (dia); opalescent glass with shaded pink lining and applied tooled amber handles.

**47**
BASKET, late 19th century
Probably England
8 x 8 x5; vertical-rib patterned pale pink glass with tooled and twisted amber handle and applied branches, leaves, and flowers in amber, white, and colorless glass. (Fig. 14)

**48**
BASKET, late 19th century
Probably England
9 x 7¼ x 6; pale rose glass with colorless handle terminating in tooled leaves and berries.

**49**
BASKET, late 19th century
Possibly England or Austria
6½ x 5¼ x 6; shaded red to pale pink glass with white outer casing and applied colorless glass handle and edge. (Fig. 14)

**50**
FOOTED BASKET, late 19th century
Probably England
8¾ x 7¼ x 6¾; copper-colored metallic splashes on white with red lining, applied colorless glass handle and foot.

**51**
BASKET, late 19th century
Probably England
4¼ x 4¾ (dia); transparent pink glass with applied colorless glass handle.

**52**
BASKET, late 19th century
Probably England
8¼ x 6 (dia); opalescent glass with applied yellow-green tooled handle and pink and yellow-green floral decoration. (Fig. 14)

**53**
BASKET, late 19th century
Probably Midwestern United States
6 x 6 (dia); white and yellow spangled glass with applied colorless glass tooled handle.

**54**
BASKET, late 19th century
Probably Austria
5¾ x 5¾ (dia); mottled pink and brown cased over white with outer casing of colorless glass, applied colorless glass tooled handle.

**55**
BASKET, late 19th century
Probably Austria
7⅝ x 5¼ x 5¾; deep red swirls on white with outer casing of colorless glass, applied colorless glass tooled handle.

## MISCELLANEOUS EUROPEAN GLASS

**56**
VASE, late 19th century
Probably Austria
5¾ x 5¾ (dia); vertical-rib patterned colorless glass with yellow and pink iridescence and applied grape and leaf decoration in blue and purple iridescent green glass.

**57**
VASE, late 19th century
Probably Austria
4¼ x 5¼ (dia); vertical-rib patterned colorless glass with yellow and pink iridescence and applied grape and leaf decoration in blue and purple iridescent green glass.

**58**
BOWL, late 19th century
Possibly Loetz, Austria
3½ x 9 (dia); ruby-to-colorless inverted thumbprint patterned glass with frosted splotches and shaded iridescence outside.

**59**
COVERED JAR, early 20th century
Possibly Loetz, Austria
8⅞ x 6⅛ x 5⅜; gold lustre decoration in draped pattern on iridescent amethyst glass with silver-plated lid and handle.

**60**
VASE, early 20th century
Possibly Loetz, Austria
10¾ x 4¼ (dia); shaded purple iridescent green glass with brown and white threaded leaf decoration.

**61**
FLOWER-FORM VASE, early 20th century
Probably Loetz, Austria
12⅞ x 5 (dia); shaded iridescent colorless glass with amber splotches.

**62**
VASE, early 20th century
"STEUBEN" engraved on bottom (spurious)
Probably Loetz, Austria
4 x 6 (dia); colorless glass with frosted amber splotches and shaded iridescent decoration.

**63**
VASE, early 20th century
Possibly Loetz, Austria
6¼ x 6¼ (dia); opaque white glass with mottled iridescent green swag or looped decoration, reddish-orange lining, applied blue lip, and applied shaded iridescent blue feet. (Fig. 49)

**64**
VASE, early 20th century
Tiffany paper label on bottom (spurious)
Possibly Loetz, Austria

6¼ x 8½ (dia); shaded gold and purple iridescent blue-green glass with blue and white swirled decoration.

**65**
VASE, late 19th to early 20th century
Attributed to J. Loetz Witwe, Austria
3¼ x 4 (dia); blue and yellow iridescent amber glass with silver overlay decoration. (Fig. 22)

**66**
LAMP, early 20th century
Venice, Italy
13 x 4½ (dia); green, yellow, white, blue, and purple millefiori cased over colorless glass with brass fittings. (Fig. 23)

**67**
VASE, early 20th century
Probably Europe
13½ x 4¾ (dia); opalescent glass with applied handles.

**68**
PAIR OF VASES, mid 19th century
Probably Bohemia
12¼ x 4⅞ (dia); painted and gilded opalescent glass. (Fig. 12)

**69**
VASE, late 19th century
Europe or United States
5 x 4½ (dia); painted and gilded opal glass in matte finish. (Fig. 43)

**70**
COMPOTE, late 19th to early 20th century
Probably Europe
4 x 6¼ (dia); pale blue glass with dark bluish-green thread at edge and dark bluish-green (appearing black) stem and foot.

**71**
COMPOTE CENTERPIECE, early 20th century
Probably Continental Europe
10 x 9¼ (dia); colorless glass bowl with trailings of blue and green, vertical-rib patterned colorless glass stem and foot with applied green thread around base.

**72**
VASE, early 20th century
Continental Europe
4¼ x 4¼ x 4⅛; pale-pink to pale-blue stained colorless glass.

**73**
PAIR OF VASES, late 19th century
Continental Europe, probably Bohemia
9½ x 4⅜ (dia); frosted colorless glass with Homeric helmeted head in oval medallion and foliate decoration in ruby stain with gilt highlights.

**74**
WATER PITCHER AND FOUR TUMBLERS, early 20th century
Probably Europe
Pitcher: 8¼ x 7⅜ x 6½, tumblers: 4⅜ x 2½ (dia); frosted tan glass with enamel and gilt floral decoration.

**75**
COVERED PUNCH BOWL, LADLE, AND NINE CUPS, 1850-1900
Continental Europe, possibly Bohemia
Bowl: 14¾ x 8¾ (dia), ladle: 12½ x 3⅛ x 5¼, cup: 3⅜ x 3⅛ x 2⅛ (dia); ruby-stained colorless glass with enameled floral sprays on alternate gold and silver vertical-striped panels. (Fig. 13)

**76**
PANELED VASE, late 19th century
Probably Bohemia
12¾ x 4 x 4; cut green glass with gilded lattice and grape-leaf borders.

**77**
COVERED BUTTER DISH, late 19th to early 20th century
Continental Europe
6¼ x 7 (dia); white and cranberry splotched transparent pale yellow glass. (Fig. 19)

**78**
PITCHER, late 19th to early 20th century
United States or Europe
8⅜ x 7¾ x 6½; thumbprint patterned marbleized glass with applied colorless glass handle. (Fig. 19)

**79**
OVAL TRAY, late 19th to early 20th century
Continental Europe
¾ x 9⅞ x 7⅜; tortoise-shell glass.

**80**
VASE, late 19th to early 20th century
Continental Europe
5¼ x 5⅞ (dia); tortoise-shell glass.

**81**
PAIR OF VASES, late 19th century
Continental Europe or United States
8½ x 4 (dia); white glass with multi-colored splashes cased in vertical-rib patterned colorless glass.

**82**
VASE, 20th century
Probably Venice, Italy or United States
13⅝ x 4¾ (dia); white and green, blue, and pink filigrees in colorless glass with crackled gold-leaf black glass base, rim, and applied decoration.

**83**
CAT-TAIL VASE, late 19th century
Europe, possibly Loetz, Austria
9½ x 4 (dia); blown colorless glass shading to purple at top with whimsical tooled decoration.

## BURMESE GLASS

**84**
SALT AND PEPPER SHAKERS, 1883-1894
Attributed to Mount Washington Glass Company, New Bedford, MA
4 x 1⅝ (dia); pressed Burmese glass with melon ribbing in matte finish, pewter caps.

**85**

TOOTHPICK HOLDER, 1883-1894
Possibly Mount Washington Glass Company, New Bedford, MA
2½ x 2⅝ (dia); blown Burmese glass with ruffled rim in matte finish.

**86**

TOOTHPICK HOLDER, 1883-1894
Attributed to Mount Washington Glass Company, New Bedford, MA
2⅝ x 1¾ x 1¾; diamond-quilted patterned Burmese glass in matte finish.

**87**

TUMBLER, 1883-1894
Attributed to Mount Washington Glass Company, New Bedford, MA
3¾ x 2⅝ (dia); Burmese glass in matte finish.

**88**

TUMBLER, 1883-1894
Attributed to Mount Washington Glass Company, New Bedford, MA
3¾ x 2¾ (dia); Burmese glass in matte finish.

**89**

LILY OR TRUMPET VASE, 1883-1894
Attributed to Mount Washington Glass Company, New Bedford, MA
8 x 3½ (dia); Burmese glass in matte finish.

**90**

LILY OR TRUMPET VASE, 1883-1894
Attributed to Mount Washington Glass Company, New Bedford, MA
7 x 3¼ (dia); Burmese glass in matte finish.

**91**

LILY OR TRUMPET VASE, 1883-1894
Attributed to Mount Washington Glass Company, New Bedford, MA
14½ x 5 (dia); Burmese glass in matte finish, brass collar repair at base.

**92**

LILY OR TRUMPET VASE, 1883-1894
Attributed to Mount Washington Glass Company, New Bedford, MA
14⅜ x 5⅜ (dia); Burmese glass in matte finish.

**93**

TOOTHPICK HOLDER, 1883-1894
Attributed to Mount Washington Glass Company, New Bedford, MA
2⅝ x 3 (dia); diamond-quilted patterned Burmese glass with yellow tooled-scroll band applied below ruffled rim in glossy finish. (Fig. 36)

**94**

VASE, 1883-1894
Attributed to Mount Washington Glass Company, New Bedford, MA
3 x 2¾ (dia); hobnail (?) patterned Burmese glass with tooled-scroll band applied below scalloped rim in glossy finish.

**95**

GEMEL OR DOUBLE BOTTLE, late 19th century
England
9½ x 4½ (dia); Queen's Burmese glass in matte finish. (Fig. 37)

**96**

DOUBLE FAIRY LAMP AND BUD VASE CENTER-PIECE, late 19th century
"CLARKE'S PATENT FAIRY LAMPS" around top of stem; "S. CLARK TRADE MARK FAIRY" on bottom of liner; and "CLARKE'S TRADE MARK CRICKLITE" on bottom of base
England
10½ x 9⅝ x 6; Queen's Burmese glass in matte finish, colorless pressed glass "Clarke" bases and liners, and gilded metal stand.

**97**

TRIPLE FAIRY LAMP AND BUD VASE CENTERPIECE, late 19th century
"S CLARK / PATENT TRADE MARK / FAIRY" on inside bottom of base and liner
England
9 x 10¾ (dia); Queen's Burmese glass in matte finish, colorless pressed glass "Clarke" liners, and gilded metal stand. (Fig. 38)

**98**

FAIRY LAMP, late 19th century
"S. CLARK / PATENT TRADE MARK / FAIRY" on inside bottom; "QUEEN'S BURMESE WARE / THOS WEBB & SONS / PATENTED" on outside bottom of base; "S. CLARK / PATENT TRADE MARK / FAIRY" on inside bottom of liner
Thomas Webb & Sons, Stourbridge, England
5⅝ x 6⅜ (dia); Queen's Burmese glass in matte finish, ruffled rim around Burmese glass base and colorless pressed glass "Clarke" liner.

**99**

FAIRY LAMP, late 19th century
"CLARKE'S TRADE MARK CRICKLITE" on inside bottom of base
England
5 x 4 (dia); Queen's Burmese glass in matte finish, colorless pressed glass base.

**100**

VASE, late 19th century
England
2¾ x 2⅝ (dia); Queen's Burmese glass bulbous body with crimped top in matte finish.

**101**

VASE, late 19th century
"QUEEN'S BURMESE WARE / THOS WEBB & SONS / PATENTED / RD80167" on bottom
Thomas Webb & Sons, Stourbridge, England
2½ x 3¾ (dia); Queen's Burmese glass with nine-sided top in matte finish.

**102**

VASE, late 19th century
"QUEEN'S BURMESE WARE / THOS WEBB & SONS

/ PATENTED / RD8018" impressed in bottom
Thomas Webb & Sons, Stourbridge, England
2½ x 3¼ (dia); Queen's Burmese glass with seven-sided top in matte finish. (Fig. 37)

**103**
VASE, late 19th century
Attributed to Thomas Webb & Sons, Stourbridge, England
3½ x 2⅝ (dia); Queen's Burmese glass with ruffled top in matte finish with painted floral decoration.

**104**
PAIR OF VASES, late 19th century
"QUEEN'S BURMESE WARE / THOS WEBB & SONS / PATENTED" on bottom
Thomas Webb & Sons, Stourbridge, England
7¾ x 3⅝ (dia); Queen's Burmese glass in matte finish with painted floral decoration. (Fig. 37)

**105**
INSERT, late 19th century
Attributed to Thomas Webb & Sons, Stourbridge, England
1½ x 3 (dia); Queen's Burmese glass with tooled band applied below rim in glossy finish and enameled floral decoration.

**106**
SUGAR BOWL, late 19th century
Possibly England
4½ x 5¾ x 3½; diamond-quilted patterned Burmese glass with square top and applied yellow handles in glossy finish.

**107**
PAIR OF VASES, late 19th century
Probably Continental Europe
4 x 3 (dia); swirled-rib patterned Burmese glass with hexagonal top in matte finish.

**108**
CREAMER, late 19th century
Probably Murano, Italy
3¾ x 4 x 2¾; Burmese glass with applied yellow handle in glossy finish.

**109**
FOOTED BOWL, 1952-1957
Attributed to Gundersen-Pairpoint Glass Works, New Bedford, MA
4⅛ x 7 (dia); Burmese glass with applied tooled feet in matte finish.

**110**
FOOTED PITCHER, 1952-1957
Attributed to Gundersen-Pairpoint Glass Works, New Bedford, MA
7¾ x 6⅛ x 4½; Burmese glass with applied tooled feet and yellow handle in matte finish.

**111**
CREAMER, 1952-1957
Attributed to Gundersen-Pairpoint Glass Works, New Bedford, MA
4⅝ x 4⅝ x 3½; diamond-quilted patterned Burmese glass with applied yellow handle in matte finish.

**112**
CREAMER, 1952-1957

Attributed to Gundersen-Pairpoint Glass Works, New Bedford, MA
4½ x 4⅝ x 3⅜; Burmese glass with applied yellow handle in matte finish.

**113**
CRUET, 1952-1957
Attributed to Gundersen-Pairpoint Glass Works, New Bedford, MA
5¾ x 3½ x 3¾; Burmese glass with applied pink handle in matte finish.

**114**
VASE, 1952-1957
Attributed to Gundersen-Pairpoint Glass Works, New Bedford, MA
8⅝ x 6 (dia); Burmese glass with flared scalloped rim in glossy finish.

**115**
VASE, 1952-1957
Probably Gundersen-Pairpoint Glass Works, New Bedford, MA
6 x 6¾ (dia); Burmese glass with flared scalloped rim in glossy finish.

**116**
FOOTED VASE, 1952-1957
Probably Gundersen-Pairpoint Glass Works, New Bedford, MA
7⅜ x 8½ x 6½; vertical-rib patterned Burmese glass ovoid bowl with ruffled top and applied yellow decoration in glossy finish. (Fig. 36)

## CORALENE GLASS

**117**
VASE, 1880-1894
Probably Mount Washington Glass Company, New Bedford, MA
7¾ x 3⅝ (dia); pink shaded to blue satin glass with raised yellow glass beads applied in dotted motifs enclosed in diamond panels, white lining, and gilded lip. (Fig. 21)

**118**
VASE, 1880-1894
Probably Mount Washington Glass Company, New Bedford, MA
7¾ x 3¾ (dia); red shaded to pale pink satin glass with raised yellow glass beads applied in coral motif, white lining, and gilded lip. (Fig. 21)

**119**
PAIR OF VASES, 1880-1894
Probably Mount Washington Glass Company, New Bedford, MA
8 x 3⅝ (dia); red shaded to pale pink satin glass with green and colorless glass beads applied in coral motif, white lining, and gilded lip. (Fig. 21)

**120**
VASE, late 19th century
England or United States
9 x 5¾ (dia); rainbow striped satin glass with yellow glass beads applied in coral motif, white lining, and gilded lip. (Fig. 21)

**121**
VASE, late 19th or 20th century
Europe or United States
7 x 3⅛ (dia); translucent white glass stained blue at base with spurious yellow glass beads applied in coral motif.

**122**
VASE, late 19th or 20th century
Europe or United States
7¾ x 4¾ (dia); translucent white glass stained pink and crimped at top with spurious yellow beads applied in coral motif.

## PEACH BLOW GLASS

**123**
BOWL, 1886-1894
Attributed to Mount Washington Glass Company, New Bedford, MA
2¼ x 4½ (dia); pink shaded to pale blue peach blow glass with scalloped top in matte finish.

**124**
COLOGNE BOTTLE WITH STOPPER, 1886-1894
Attributed to Mount Washington Glass Company, New Bedford, MA
5½ x 1⅝ (dia); pink shaded to pale blue mold-blown peach blow glass in vertical-rib pattern in matte finish with painted floral decoration and facet-cut stopper.

**125**
PAIR OF TUMBLERS, 1886-1894
Attributed to Mount Washington Glass Company, New Bedford, MA
3¾ x 2⅝ (dia); pink shaded to pale blue peach blow glass in matte finish.

**126**
BOWL, 1886-1888
Attributed to New England Glass Company, East Cambridge, MA
4 x 8⅝ (dia); deep red shaded to white peach blow glass in matte finish with scalloped top. (Fig. 39)

**127**
PAIR OF TUMBLERS, 1886-1888
Attributed to New England Glass Company, East Cambridge, MA
3¼ x 2½ (dia); deep red shaded to white peach blow glass in matte finish. (Fig. 39)

**128**
VASE, 1886-1888
Attributed to New England Glass Company, East Cambridge, MA
8½ x 4 (dia); deep red shaded to white peach blow glass in matte finish. (Fig. 39)

**129**
SUGAR BOWL, 1886-1888
Attributed to New England Glass Company, East Cambridge, MA
2¾ x 5½ x 3¾; deep red shaded to white peach blow glass with applied white handles in glossy finish.

**130**
LILY TRUMPET VASE, 1886-1888
Attributed to New England Glass Company, East Cambridge, MA
5¾ x 2¾ (dia); deep red shaded to white peach blow glass in glossy finish.

**131**
LILY TRUMPET VASE, 1886-1888
Attributed to New England Glass Company, East Cambridge, MA
18⅛ x 6¼ (dia); deep red shaded to white peach blow glass in glossy finish.

**132**
VASE, 1886-1888
Attributed to the Boston and Sandwich Glass Company, Sandwich, MA
3¾ x 3⅜ (dia); pink shaded to pale blue peach blow glass with crimped top in matte finish.

**133**
VASE, 1886-1888
Attributed to the Boston and Sandwich Glass Company, Sandwich, MA
4⅞ x 3¼ (dia); pink peach blow glass with crimped and folded top lined at rim with colorless glass in matte finish.

**134**
BOWL, 1886-c. 1890
Possibly Hobbs, Brockunier & Company, Wheeling, WV
2¾ x 5⅛ (dia); red shaded to yellow mold-blown peach blow glass in glossy finish with white lining and colorless outer casing.

**135**
CREAMER, 1886-c. 1890
Possibly Hobbs, Brockunier & Company, Wheeling, WV
4¼ x 4⅜ x 4¾; deep red shaded to yellow peach blow glass in glossy finish with bluish-white lining and applied amber handle.

**136**
PITCHER, 1886-c. 1890
Possibly Hobbs, Brockunier & Company, Wheeling, WV
5¼ x 5½ x 4¾; deep red shaded to orange peach blow glass in glossy finish with white lining and applied amber handle.

**137**
PAIR OF LAMP SHADES, 1886-c. 1890
Possibly Hobbs, Brockunier & Company, Wheeling, WV
6¼ x 7½ (dia); red shaded to yellow peach blow glass in glossy finish with white lining.

**138**
TUMBLER, 1886-c. 1890
Possibly Hobbs, Brockunier & Company, Wheeling, WV
3¾ x 2¾ (dia); deep red shaded to yellow peach blow glass in glossy finish with white lining and colorless outer casing.

**139**
PAIR OF "MORGAN" VASES WITH STANDS, c. 1886

Attributed to Hobbs, Brockunier & Company, Wheeling, WV
10 x 3⅛ (dia; vase: 8 x 3 dia, stand: 3¼ x 3⅛ dia); deep red shaded to yellow peach blow glass in matte finish with white lining, pressed amber glass stands. (Fig. 40, cover)

**140**
VASE, 1886-c. 1890
Possibly Hobbs, Brockunier & Company, Wheeling, WV
10½ x 5½ (dia); red shaded to yellow peach blow glass in matte finish with white lining.

**141**
FOOTED BOWL, 1952-1957
Attributed to Gundersen-Pairpoint Glass Works, New Bedford, MA
3½ x 4⅞ (dia); pink shaded to white peach blow glass in matte finish.

**142**
FOOTED BOWL, mid 20th century
Attributed to Gundersen-Pairpoint Glass Works, New Bedford, MA or Venice, Italy
2¾ x 3⅝ x 2¾ (dia); pink shaded to pale blue peach blow glass with applied pale blue tooled berries at sides in matte finish.

**143**
PAIR OF CANDLESTICKS, 1952-1957
Attributed to Gundersen-Pairpoint Glass Works, New Bedford, MA
7¾ x 2¾ (dia); pink shaded to white vertical-rib and diamond patterned peach blow glass in matte finish. (Fig. 41)

**144**
CREAMER, 1952-1957
Attributed to Gundersen-Pairpoint Glass Works, New Bedford, MA
2¾ x 3½ (dia); pink shaded to pale blue peach blow glass with applied pale blue handle in matte finish.

**145**
CUP AND SAUCER, 1952-1957
Attributed to Gundersen-Pairpoint Glass Works, New Bedford, MA
Cup: 3¼ x 4¾ x 3⅞ (dia), saucer: 1 x 5½ (dia); pink shaded to pale blue swirled peach blow glass with applied pale pink handle in matte finish. (Fig. 41)

**146**
SMALL PITCHER, 1952-1957
Attributed to Gundersen-Pairpoint Glass Works, New Bedford, MA
5¼ x 3¼ x 2⅛ (dia); pink shaded to white peach blow glass with applied white handle in matte finish.

**147**
PAIR OF GOBLETS, 1952-1957
Attributed to Gundersen-Pairpoint Glass Works, New Bedford, MA
6½ x 3½ (dia); pink shaded to white peach blow glass in matte finish.

**148**
SAUCER WITH HANDLE, 1952-1957
Attributed to Gundersen-Pairpoint Glass Works, New Bedford, MA

2½ x 5½ x 3½ (dia); pink shaded to white peach blow glass with applied white handle in matte finish. (Fig. 41)

**149**
PLATE, 1952-1957
Attributed to Gundersen-Pairpoint Glass Works, New Bedford, MA
1 x 7⅞ (dia); pink shaded to white peach blow glass in matte finish.

**150**
VASE, 1952-1957
Attributed to Gundersen-Pairpoint Glass Works, New Bedford, MA
4½ x 5 (dia); pink shaded to pale blue vertical-rib patterned peach blow glass with scalloped top in matte finish.

**151**
VASE, 1952-1957
Attributed to Gundersen-Pairpoint Glass Works, New Bedford, MA
4 x 2⅝ (dia); pink shaded to white peach blow glass in matte finish.

## POMONA GLASS

**152**
CELERY VASE, 1885-1888
Attributed to New England Glass Company, East Cambridge, MA
6½ x 4¼ (dia); Pomona glass with amber and blue stain highlights. (Fig. 33)

**153**
CELERY VASE, 1885-1888
Attributed to New England Glass Company, East Cambridge, MA
5¼ x 3¼ (dia); Pomona glass with amber and blue stain highlights. (Fig. 33)

**154**
CRUET WITH STOPPER, 1885-1888
Attributed to New England Glass Company, East Cambridge, MA
5½ x 3¾ (dia); Pomona glass with amber and traces of blue stain highlights. (Fig. 33)

**155**
FINGERBOWL AND PLATE, 1885-1888
Attributed to New England Glass Company, East Cambridge, MA
Bowl: 2½ x 5¼ (dia), plate: 1¼ x 6⅝ (dia); Pomona glass with amber stain highlights.

**156**
PITCHER, 1885-1888
Attributed to New England Glass Company, East Cambridge, MA
7¼ x 5¾ x 4⅛; Pomona glass with amber stain highlights.

**157**
PITCHER, 1885-1888
Attributed to New England Glass Company, East Cambridge, MA
8 x 7¾ x 6½; Pomona glass with amber stain highlights.

**158**
PITCHER, 1885-1888
Attributed to New England Glass Company, East Cambridge, MA
7 x 8 x 6¼; Pomona glass with amber and blue stain highlights. (Fig. 33)

**159**
PAIR OF BOWLS AND PLATES, 1885-1888
Attributed to New England Glass Company, East Cambridge, MA
Bowl: 2 x 3½ (dia), plate: ⅞ x 4¼ (dia); Pomona glass with amber stain highlights.

**160**
PAIR OF TUMBLERS, 1885-1888
Attributed to New England Glass Company, East Cambridge, MA
4 x 2½ (dia); Pomona glass with amber and blue stain highlights. (Fig. 33)

## AMBERINA GLASS

**161**
SYRUP PITCHER AND PLATE, 1883-1888
"James W. Tufts / Boston / warranted / quadruple plated" stamped into bottom of plate
Attributed to New England Glass Company, East Cambridge, MA
Pitcher: 5⅞ x 4⅜ x 3¼, plate: ¾ x 5¾ (dia); Plated Amberina glass with lighter-colored ribs and opalescent lining, silver-plated mounts and plate. (Fig. 34, cover)

**162**
FINGER BOWL, 1883-1888
Attributed to New England Glass Company, East Cambridge, MA
2¾ x 5¼ (dia); Amberina glass.

**163**
FINGER BOWL, 1883-1888
Attributed to New England Glass Company, East Cambridge, MA
2⅝ x 4⅛ (dia); inverted-thumbprint patterned Amberina glass.

**164**
FINGER BOWL, 1883-1888
Attributed to New England Glass Company, East Cambridge, MA
2½ x 5⅛ (dia); Amberina glass with scalloped top.

**165**
PAIR OF LEMONADE GLASSES, 1883-1888
Attributed to New England Glass Company, East Cambridge, MA
3¾ x 3¼ x 2½ (dia); "optic"-ribbed Amberina glass. (Fig. 32)

**166**
TOOTHPICK HOLDER, 1883-1888
Attributed to New England Glass Company, East Cambridge, MA
2⅛ x 2½ (dia); diamond-quilted patterned Amberina glass with triangular-fold top.

**167**
WHISKEY GLASS, 1883-1888
Attributed to New England Glass Company, East Cambridge, MA
2¾ x 2 (dia); diamond-quilted patterned Amberina glass.

**168**
WHISKEY GLASS, 1883-1888
Attributed to New England Glass Company, East Cambridge, MA
2½ x 2⅛ (dia); diamond-quilted patterned Amberina glass. (Fig. 32)

**169**
WHISKEY GLASS, 1883-1888
Attributed to New England Glass Company, East Cambridge, MA
2⅝ x 2⅛ (dia); diamond-quilted patterned Amberina glass. (Fig. 32)

**170**
PITCHER, 1883-1888
Probably New England Glass Company, East Cambridge, MA
7¾ x 7½ x 6 (dia); diamond-quilted patterned Amberina glass in reversed colors with applied colorless handle. (Fig. 32)

**171**
BASKET, 1883-1888
Probably New England Glass Company, East Cambridge, MA
6 x 5½ (dia); "optic"-rib patterned Amberina glass.

**172**
VASE, 1888-c. 1917
"Amberina / Libbey" acid stamp on bottom
Libbey Glass Company, Toledo, OH
13¾ x 5¾ (dia); "optic"-rib patterned Amberina glass with scalloped top.

**173**
TOOTHPICK HOLDER, 1880s
Probably Midwestern United States
3 x 1⅞ (dia); inverted-thumbprint patterned Amberina glass.

**174**
TOOTHPICK HOLDER, c. 1886
Attributed to Hobbs, Brockunier & Company, Wheeling, WV
2¾ x 2¼ (dia); pressed Amberina glass in daisy and button pattern.

**175**
PAIR OF TUMBLERS, 1880s
Probably United States
3¾ x 2½ (dia); swirled-rib patterned Amberina glass.

**176**
TUMBLER, 1880s
Probably United States
3¾ x 2½ (dia); swirled-rib patterned Amberina glass.

**177**
TUMBLER, 1880s
Probably United States
3¾ x 2½ (dia); panel-rib patterned Amberina glass. (Fig. 32)

**178**
TUMBLER, 1880s
Probably United States
3¾ x 2¾ (dia); panel-rib patterned Amberina glass.

**179**
TUMBLER, 1880s
Probably United States
3¾ x 2½ (dia); swirled-rib patterned Amberina glass.
(Fig. 32)

**180**
VASE, 1880s
Probably United States
10 x 3⅛ (dia); vertical-rib patterned Amberina glass with
applied spiral of pincered amber decoration.

**181**
LILY VASE, 1880s
Probably United States
7⅛ x 3½ (dia); "optic"-rib patterned Amberina glass.

**182**
LILY VASE, 1880s
Probably United States
7 x 3⅛ (dia); Amberina glass.

**183**
LILY VASE, 1880s
Probably United States
7⅛ x 3¼ (dia); "optic"-rib patterned Amberina glass.

**184**
PAIR OF TRUMPET VASES, 1880s
Probably United States
7 x 4½ (dia); "optic"-rib patterned Amberina glass with
crimped top.

**185**
BOWL, 1880s
Probably United States
3½ x 9⅞ (dia); inverted-thumbprint patterned Amberina
glass.

**186**
WINE GLASS, 1880s
Probably United States
4½ x 2⅜ (dia); "optic"-rib patterned Amberina glass.

**187**
PAIR OF LILAC OR TRUMPET VASES, late 19th century
Probably Stourbridge, England
6¼ x 2½ (dia); vertical-rib patterned Amberina glass with
translucent opalescent outer casing and colorless glass foot.

**188**
FOOTED VASE, late 19th century
Probably England
9¼ x 5¾ (dia); "optic"-rib patterned Amberina glass with
crimped top, applied pale yellow tooled-scroll band, and
crimped foot.

**189**
BOWL, late 19th century
Probably England
3⅛ x 9¼ (dia); diamond patterned Amberina glass with
scalloped top.

## AGATA AND OPAQUE GREEN GLASS

**190**
TUMBLER, c. 1887
Attributed to New England Glass Company, East Cambridge,
MA
3⅞ x 2½ (dia); deep red shaded to white Agata glass with
mottled yellow metallic stain in glossy finish.

**191**
FINGER BOWL, c. 1887
Attributed to New England Glass Company, East Cambridge,
MA
2½ x 5⅛ (dia); deep red shaded to pale pink Agata glass
with spattered yellow metallic stain in glossy finish, scalloped top.

**192**
"OPAQUE GREEN" CUP WITH HANDLE, c. 1887
Attributed to New England Glass Company, East Cambridge,
MA
2⅝ x 3¼ x 2⅝ (dia); matte translucent green glass with
mottled blue metallic stain and traces of gilt around top.
(Fig. 35)

## MOUNT WASHINGTON GLASS,
## SPECIAL TYPES

**193**
COVERED BISCUIT OR COOKIE JAR, c. 1893
"Crown Milano / MT. W. G. Co" label on bottom
Mount Washington Glass Company, New Bedford, MA
5 x 5⅜ (dia); painted opal glass with silver-plated cover,
rim, and bail handle.

**194**
COVERED BISCUIT OR COOKIE JAR, c. 1894
"PMC" in diamond and "3931" in red on bottom
Mount Washington Glass Company, Pairpoint Manufacturing Company, New Bedford, MA
6½ x 7¼ (dia); Royal Flemish glass with silver-plated cover,
rim, and bail handle. (Fig. 42)

**195**
COVERED BISCUIT OR COOKIE JAR, 1890s
Attributed to Mount Washington Glass Company, New
Bedford, MA
7½ x 5¼ (dia); Royal Flemish glass with silver-plated cover,
rim, and bail handle. (Fig. 43)

**196**
COVERED BISCUIT OR COOKIE JAR, 1890s
Attributed to Mount Washington Glass Company, New
Bedford, MA
8¼ x 5¼ (dia); Royal Flemish glass with silver-plated cover,
rim, and bail handle. (Fig. 42)

**197**
COVERED BISCUIT OR COOKIE JAR, 1890s
Possibly Mount Washington Glass Company, New Bedford,
MA
7½ x 5½ (dia); painted opal glass, silver-plated metal cover
and rim.

**198**
COVERED BISCUIT OR COOKIE JAR, 1890s
Possibly Mount Washington Glass Company, New Bedford, MA
8 x 5½ (dia); painted opal glass, brass and silver-plated metal mounts and bail handle.

**199**
COVERED BISCUIT OR COOKIE JAR, 1890s
"3930 / 232" in green on bottom
Probably Mount Washington Glass Company, New Bedford, MA
6 x 7¼ (dia); painted opal glass with silver-plated cover, rim, and bail handle.

**200**
COVERED BISCUIT OR COOKIE JAR, 1890s
Possibly New England
5¾ x 6¾ (dia); painted opal glass with applied glass beads, silver-plated cover, rim, and bail handle. (Fig. 43, cover)

**201**
BRIDE'S BASKET OR BERRY BOWL IN STAND, late 19th century
Attributed to Mount Washington Glass Company, New Bedford, MA
13¾ x 9¾ x 9 (basket: 4½ x 9¾ x 8¼); acid-etched pink casing over white "Mount Washington Cameo" glass, silver-plated stand marked "James Tufts, Boston." (Fig. 44)

**202**
LAMP SHADE, late 19th century
Attributed to Mount Washington Glass Company, New Bedford, MA
5¼ x 8⅛ (dia); acid-etched pink casing over white "Mount Washington Cameo" glass.

**203**
PAIR OF VASES, late 19th century
Attributed to Mount Washington Glass Company, New Bedford, MA
10½ x 5¾ (dia); acid-etched pink casing over white "Mount Washington Cameo" glass. (Fig. 44)

**204**
PAIR OF SALT SHAKERS, late 19th century
Attributed to Mount Washington Glass Company, New Bedford, MA
2¾ x 2¼ (dia); molded pink satin glass with painted floral decoration and white-metal caps.

## STEUBEN GLASS

**205**
PAIR OF CANDLESTICKS, 1920-1930
"STEUBEN" fleur-de-lis paper label and acid stamp on bottom of one
Steuben Division of Corning Glass Works, Corning, NY
10 x 5⅜ (dia); acid-etched Jade Green cased over Alabaster glass in "Chinese" pattern. (Fig. 58)

**206**
VASE, 1920-1930
Attributed to Steuben Division of Corning Glass Works, Corning, NY
9½ x 7⅜ (dia); acid-etched Jade Green cased over Alabaster glass in "dragon" pattern. (Fig. 58)

**207**
VASE, 1920-1930
Attributed to Steuben Division of Corning Glass Works, Corning, NY
8 x 5¼ (dia); acid-etched Jade Green cased over Jade Yellow glass in "chrysanthemum" pattern.

**208**
BOWL, 1920-1930
Attributed to Steuben Division of Corning Glass Works, Corning, NY
4⅜ x 11¾ (dia); Jade Green glass.

**209**
FOOTED BOWL, 1920-1930
Attributed to Steuben Division of Corning Glass Works, Corning, NY
5 x 12 (dia); swirled-rib patterned light Topaz (pale yellow) glass with pale Pomona Green foot with folded rim. (Fig. 61)

**210**
PAIR OF PLATES, 1920-1930
"STEUBEN" acid stamp on bottom of each
Steuben Division of Corning Glass Works, Corning, NY
½ x 8⅝ (dia); swirled-rib patterned Celeste Blue glass. (Fig. 61)

**211**
PLATE, 1920-1930
"STEUBEN / F. Carder" engraved on bottom
Frederick Carder, Steubn Division of Corning Glass Works, Corning, NY
⅝ x 8½ (dia); opaque black glass with Jade Green threaded edge.

**212**
COMPOTE, 1920-1930
"STEUBEN" acid stamp on bottom
Steuben Division of Corning Glass Works, Corning, NY
8 x 8½ (dia); "optic"-rib patterned colorless glass with green wafer between bowl and stem.

**213**
VASE, late 1920s
Attributed to Steuben Division of Corning Glass Works, Corning, NY
6¾ x 6¾ (dia); "optic"-rib patterned colorless glass with two green glass rings around upper portion.

**214**
VASE, 1920-1930
"STEUBEN" fleur-de-lis acid stamp on bottom
Steuben Division of Corning Glass Works, Corning, NY
6⅞ x 6½ (dia); "optic"-rib patterned French Blue glass with two blue glass rings around upper portion.

**215**
VASE, 1920-1930
Attributed to Steuben Division of Corning Glass Works, Corning, NY
6⅞ x 6⅞ (dia); swirled-rib patterned Bristol Yellow glass with flared rim. (Fig. 61)

**216**
VASE, 1920-1930
"STEUBEN" fleur-de-lis acid stamp on bottom
Steuben Division of Corning Glass Works, Corning, NY
7½ x 6¾ (dia); "ogee" patterned Bristol Yellow glass with black threads applied under rim.

**217**
"GROTESQUE" BOWL, late 1920s to early 1930s
"Steuben" acid stamp on bottom
Steuben Division of Corning Glass Works, Corning, NY
6 x 11 x 6⅞; rib-molded, flared, and shaped colorless glass shaded to Flemish Blue at top. (Fig. 62)

**218**
COLOGNE BOTTLE, late 1920s
"STEUBEN" fleur-de-lis acid stamp on bottom
Steuben Division of Corning Glass Works, Corning, NY
8½ x 4⅞ (dia); Cintra center shading from black to white cased in heavy cut colorless glass with controlled bubbles. (Fig 59)

**219**
LAMP BASE, 1920-1930
Attributed to Steuben Division of Corning Glass Works, Corning, NY
12¾ x 7¼ x 3¼; pink Cluthra glass cased in Pomona Green with applied colorless handles in matte finish and acid-etched in "Chang" pattern. (Fig. 60)

**220**
LAMP AND SHADE, c. 1915
Attributed to Steuben Glass Works, Corning, NY
Base: 8¼ x 5½ (dia), shade: 4¼ x 10½ (dia); Calcite mold-blown glass with pulled feather decoration in green and Gold Aurene. (Fig. 47)

**221**
BOWL CENTERPIECE, c. 1915
Attributed to Steuben Glass Works, Corning, NY
1½ x 14¾ (dia); Calcite glass with Gold Aurene lining. (Cover)

**222**
BOWL CENTERPIECE, c. 1915
Attributed to Steuben Glass Works, Corning, NY
2 x 12¾ (dia); Calcite glass with Gold Aurene lining.

**223**
BOWL CENTERPIECE, c. 1915
Attributed to Steuben Glass Works, Corning, NY
2¾ x 10 (dia); Calcite glass with Gold Aurene lining.

**224**
BOWL, c. 1915
Attributed to Steuben Glass Works, Corning, NY
2 X 10 (dia); Calcite glass with Gold Aurene lining.

**225**
BOWL, c. 1915
Attributed to Steuben Glass Works, Corning, NY
4⅛ x 8 (dia); Calcite glass with Gold Aurene lining.

**226**
COMPOTE, c. 1915
Attributed to Steuben Glass Works, Corning, NY
5¼ x 10¼ (dia); Calcite glass with Gold Aurene lining.

**227**
COMPOTE, c. 1915
Attributed to Steuben Glass Works, Corning, NY
5½ x 8 (dia); Calcite glass with Gold Aurene lining.

**228**
FINGERBOWL PLATE, c. 1915
Attributed to Steuben Glass Works, Corning, NY
1 x 6¼ (dia); Calcite glass with Gold Aurene lining.

**229**
PLATE, c. 1915
Attributed to Steuben Glass Works, Corning, NY
1¼ x 6⅛ (dia); Calcite glass with Gold Aurene lining.

**230**
PAIR OF SHERBETS WITH PLATES, c. 1915
Attributed to Steuben Glass Works, Corning, NY
Sherbet: 3¾ x 3⅞ (dia), plate: 1 x 6 (dia); Calcite glass with Gold Aurene lining.

**231**
BOWL, c. 1915-1918
"Aurene 2687" engraved on bottom
Steuben Glass Works, Corning, NY
5 x 10 (dia); Blue Aurene (iridescent cobalt) glass. (Fig. 55)

**232**
DARNER, 1920-1930
Attributed to Steuben Division of Corning Glass Works, Corning, NY
6½ x 2½ (dia); Blue Aurene (iridescent cobalt) glass. (Fig. 55)

**233**
VASE, c. 1910-1915
"Aurene 723" engraved on bottom
Steuben Glass Works, Corning, NY
6¼ x 6 (dia); Blue Aurene (iridescent cobalt) glass with scalloped top.

**234**
VASE, c. 1910-1915
"Aurene 723" engraved on bottom
Steuben Glass Works, Corning, NY
7 x 7 (dia); Blue Aurene (iridescent cobalt) glass with scalloped top. (Fig. 55)

**235**
"RUSTIC" VASE, 1915-1918
"Aurene 2741" engraved on bottom
Steuben Glass Works, Corning, NY
6⅜ x 3 (dia); Blue Aurene (iridescent cobalt) glass. (Fig. 55)

**236**
VASE, 1920-1930
"Aurene 5070" engraved on bottom
Steuben Division of Corning Glass Works, Corning, NY
6 x 8 (dia); Gold Aurene (iridescent amber) glass with blue shaded iridescent rim edge and foot.

**237**
PAIR OF CANDLESTICKS, 1920-1930
"Aurene 2956" engraved on bottom of each
Steuben Glass Works, Corning, NY
10 x 5⅜ (dia); Gold Aurene (iridescent amber) glass.

**238**
COLOGNE BOTTLE WITH STOPPER, 1920-1930
"Aurene 2839" engraved on bottom
Steuben Glass Works, Corning, NY
6 x 3 (dia): Gold Aurene (iridescent amber) glass.

**239**
PAIR OF SHELL COMPOTES, 1920-1930
"Aurene 2957" engraved on bottom and paper
"STEUBEN" label on bottom
Steuben Glass Works, Corning, NY
7½ x 5¾ x 3⅝; Gold Aurene (iridescent amber) glass.
(Cover)

**240**
COMPOTE, 1920-1930
"Aurene 367" engraved on bottom
Steuben Glass Works, Corning, NY
7¾ x 6¾ (dia); Gold Aurene (iridescent amber) glass with
scalloped rim.

**241**
COMPOTE, 1920-1930
"Aurene 2643" engraved on bottom
Steuben Glass Works, Corning, NY
8⅛ x 6 (dia); Gold Aurene (iridescent amber) glass.

**242**
COMPOTE, 1920-1930
"Aurene 1983" engraved on bottom
Steuben Glass Works, Corning, NY
4¼ x 6 (dia); Gold Aurene (iridescent amber) glass.

**243**
CREAMER, 1920-1930
"Aurene 252" engraved on bottom
Steuben Glass Works, Corning, NY
4 x 3⅞ x 2⅞; diamond-quilted patterned Gold Aurene
(iridescent amber) glass.

**244**
SUGAR BOWL, 1920-1930
"Aurene 252" engraved on bottom
Steuben Glass Works, Corning, NY
2½ x 3⅜; diamond-quilted patterned Gold Aurene (irides-
cent amber) glass.

**245**
LAMP, c. 1915
"STEUBEN" stamped in silver on shade
Steuben Glass Works, Corning, NY
16½ x 8½ x 5¾ (dia); bronze frame with Brown Aurene
shade. (Fig. 56)

**246**
SHERBET AND PLATE, 1920-1930
"Aurene 2361" engraved on bottom of each
Steuben Glass Works, Corning, NY
Sherbet: 3⅞ x 3⅞ (dia), plate: 1 x 6¼ (dia); Gold Aurene
(iridescent amber) glass.

**247**
THREE SHERBETS, 1920-1930
"Aurene 2680" engraved on bottom
Steuben Glass Works, Corning, NY
3⅞ x 3⅞ (dia); Gold Aurene (iridescent amber) glass.

**248**
"TUMBLE-UP" PITCHER, 1920-1930
"Aurene 3064" engraved on bottom
Steuben Glass Works, Corning, NY
6½ x 5½ x 4¾ (pitcher: 5¼ x 5½ x 4¾, tumbler: 3⅜ x
2½ dia); Gold Aurene (iridescent amber) glass.

**249**
VASE, 1920-1930
"Steuben - Aurene 6031" engraved on bottom
Steuben Division of Corning Glass Works, Corning, NY
6¾ x 6¼ (dia); swirled-rib patterned Gold Aurene (irides-
cent amber) glass.

**250**
VASE, 1920-1930
"Steuben" engraved on bottom
Steuben Glass Works, Corning, NY
5¾ x 5 (dia); swirled vertical-rib patterned Gold Aurene
(iridescent amber) glass.

**251**
VASE, 1920-1930
"Steuben" engraved on bottom
Steuben Glass Works, Corning, NY
5½ x 5¼ (dia); vertical-rib patterned Gold Aurene (irides-
cent amber) glass.

**252**
TRUMPET VASE WITH CALLA LILIES, 1920-1930
"Steuben" engraved on bottom
Steuben Division of Corning Glass Works, Corning, NY
12 x 6¾ x 5½; Ivrene (iridescent translucent white) glass.
(Fig. 57)

**253**
COLOGNE BOTTLE WITH STOPPER
"Aurene 189" engraved on bottom
Steuben Glass Works, Corning, NY
11 x 3⅛ (dia); Gold Aurene (iridescent amber) glass.

**254**
TAZZA, 1940-1960
"Steuben" engraved on bottom
Steuben Glass, Corning, NY
4⅞ x 9¾ (dia); colorless glass.

**255**
FOOT BOWL, 1940-1960
"Steuben" acid stamp on bottom
Steuben Glass, Corning, NY
8⅝ x 10 (dia); colorless glass.

## TIFFANY GLASS

**256**
OCTAGONAL VASE, 1900-1920
"103A Coll. L. C. Tiffany Favrile" engraved on bottom
Tiffany Furnaces, Corona, Long Island, NY
3¾ x 2¾ (dia); Chinese dragon cameo-carved yellow -
green Agate glass. (Fig. 53)

**257**
VASE IN STAND, 1902-c. 1920
"L.C.T." engraved on bottom, "TIFFANY STUDIOS / NEW
YORK / 1043" stamped in bottom of stand

Tiffany Furnaces and Tiffany Studios, Corona and New York, NY
15¼ x 5⅛ (dia); iridescent amber glass with green and white pulled feather decoration, brass stand. (Fig. 50)

### 258
FLORIFORM VASE, 1893-1920s
"8054 / L.C.T." engraved on bottom
Tiffany Furnaces, Corona, Long Island, NY
16 x 4¾ (dia); iridescent amber glass with red and white pulled feather decoration and white threads around bottom edge. (Fig. 50)

### 259
FLORIFORM VASE, 1893-1920s
"385 L. C. Tiffany - Favrile" engraved on bottom
Tiffany Furnaces, Corona, Long Island, NY
11⅜ x 4 (dia); translucent white glass with blue and deep red outer layer pulled up near top, applied foot of translucent white glass with pulled green thread decoration and gold iridescence on bottom. (Fig. 50)

### 260
VASE, 1893-1920s
"X2954" engraved on bottom
Attributed to Tiffany Furnaces, Corona, Long Island, NY
11½ x 4⅞ (dia); iridescent brown translucent glass with pulled blue, green, and orange thread decoration.

### 261
VASE, 1893-1920s
"2439 L. C. Tiffany - Favrile" engraved on bottom
Tiffany Furnaces, Corona, Long Island, NY
8 x 5 (dia); translucent red glass with gold iridescent lining and cobalt blue foot.

### 262
CYPRIOTE VASE, 1893-1920s
"844 T L. C. Tiffany - Favrile" engraved on bottom
Tiffany Furnaces, Corona, Long Island, NY
4¼ x 5¾ (dia); translucent yellow glass alternately cloudy-white and irregularly pitted at rim and lightly shaded purple at base. (Fig. 54)

### 263
VASE, 1893-1920s
"L.C.T. Y3059" engraved on bottom
Tiffany Furnaces, Corona, Long Island, NY
9¾ x 6¼ (dia); ribbed colorless glass encasing layers of green air-trap glass and controlled bubbles.

### 264
BOWL, 1893-1920s
"1274 L.C.T. Favrile" engraved on bottom
Tiffany Furnaces, Corona, Long Island, NY
2⅛ x 6¼ (dia); iridescent cobalt blue glass with scalloped top.

### 265
FLOWER BOWL CENTERPIECE, 1893-1920s
"384 N Louis C. Tiffany Furnaces - Inc. Favrile" engraved on bottom
Tiffany Furnaces, Corona, Long Island, NY
2 x 10¼ (dia); iridescent cobalt blue glass with green lily-pad decoration inside.

### 266
FLOWER BOWL CENTERPIECE, 1893-1920s
"6906 L L. C. Tiffany - Favrile" engraved on bottom of bowl and flower holder
Tiffany Furnaces, Corona, Long Island, NY
4¾ x 14¾ (dia); iridescent cobalt blue glass with shaded lily-pad decoration inside.

### 267
BOWL, 1893-1920s
"1277 L.C.T. Favrile" engraved on bottom
Tiffany Furnaces, Corona, Long Island, NY
2½ x 4 (dia); iridescent cobalt blue mold-blown glass with scalloped top.

### 268
LAMP AND SHADE, 1893-1920s
"L.C.T. Favrile" engraved on bottom of standard and top of shade
Tiffany Furnaces, Corona, Long Island, NY
14 x 7⅜ (dia); iridescent cobalt blue glass.

### 269
VASE, 1893-1920s
"1973 L. C. Tiffany - Favrile" engraved on bottom
Tiffany Furnaces, Corona, Long Island, NY
8¾ x 6½ (dia); iridescent cobalt blue glass.

### 270
VASE, 1893-1920s
"4305 K L. C. Tiffany - Favrile" engraved on bottom
Tiffany Furnaces, Corona, Long Island, NY
2¾ x 3½ (dia); iridescent cobalt blue glass with green leaf-and-vine decoration. (Fig. 50)

### 271
CALYX FLORIFORM VASE, 1893-1920s
"185 J L. C. Tiffany - Favrile" engraved on bottom
Tiffany Furnaces, Corona, Long Island, NY
12⅛ x 3¾ (dia); cobalt blue glass with green leaf-and-vine and thread decoration and iridescent foot. (Cover)

### 272
SET OF THREE CHAMPAGNES, 1893-1920s
"L.C.T." engraved on bottom of each
Tiffany Furnaces, Corona, Long Island, NY
6 x 3⅜ (dia); gold iridescent amber glass.

### 273
CORDIAL GLASS, 1893-1920s
"L.C.T." engraved on bottom
Tiffany Furnaces, Corona, Long Island, NY
4½ x 1¾ (dia); gold iridescent amber glass.

### 274
FINGERBOWL AND PLATE, 1893-1920s
"L.C.T." engraved on bottom of each
Tiffany Furnaces, Corona, Long Island, NY
Bowl: 2¼ x 4 (dia), plate: 1½ x 6 (dia); gold iridescent amber glass with engraved swag decoration.

### 275
PAIR OF FINGERBOWLS AND PLATES, 1893-1920s
"L.C.T." engraved on bottom of each, one set with paper "TIFFANY FAVRILE" label
Tiffany Furnaces, Corona, Long Island, NY

Bowl: 2¼ x 4¼ (dia), plate: 1 x 6 (dia); gold iridescent amber glass with pincered twists.

**276**

LAMP WITH THREE LILY SHADES, 1902-c. 1920
"TIFFANY STUDIOS / NEW YORK / 306" stamped into bottom
Tiffany Furnaces and Tiffany Studios, Corona and New York, NY
16¼ x 9 x 8¼; gold iridescent amber glass, gilded bronze frame.

**277**

PAIR OF SALT OR NUT DISHES, 1893-1920s
"L.C.T." engraved on bottom of each
Tiffany Furnaces, Corona, Long Island, NY
1⅛ x 2⅝ (dia); gold iridescent amber glass with scalloped top.

**278**

TOOTHPICK HOLDER, 1893-1920s
"L.C.T. J5509" engraved on bottom
Tiffany Furnaces, Corona, Long Island, NY
1¾ x 1½ (dia); gold iridescent amber glass with four push-ins.

**279**

SMALL BOWL, 1893-1920s
"L.C.T." engraved on bottom
Tiffany Furnaces, Corona, Long Island, NY
1⅞ x 2½ (dia); gold iridescent amber glass.

**280**

CALYX FLORIFORM VASE, 1893-1920s
"7188D L. C. Tiffany - Favrile" engraved on bottom
Tiffany Furnaces, Corona, Long Island, NY
9 x 3¼ (dia); gold iridescent amber glass with green leaf-and-vine decoration. (Fig. 50)

**281**

VASE, 1893-1920s
"A2004 L.C.T." engraved on bottom
Tiffany Furnaces, Corona, Long Island, NY
7 x 5¼ (dia); vertical-rib patterned amber glass with iridescent green and yellow wavy bands.

**282**

VASE IN WIRE HOLDER, 1893-1920s
"3259 C L.C.T. Favrile" engraved on underside of lip
Tiffany Furnaces, Corona, Long Island, NY
19½ x 4¼ (dia); gold iridescent translucent white glass with silver tip at bottom and gilded brass wire stand. (Cover)

**283**

VASE, 1893-1920s
"L.C.T. / F 1908" engraved on bottom
Tiffany Furnaces, Corona, Long Island, NY
9⅝ x 4¾ (dia); vertical-rib patterned gold iridescent amber glass with green and white floral decoration. (Fig. 50)

**284**

VASE, 1893-1920s
"691 E L. C. Tiffany - Favrile" engraved on bottom
Tiffany Furnaces, Corona, Long Island, NY
14⅜ x 3⅝ (dia); gold iridescent amber glass with green floral decoration. (Fig. 50)

**285**

VASE, 1893-1920s
"L.C.T. H1552" engraved on bottom
Tiffany Furnaces, Corona, Long Island, NY
6⅞ x 4 (dia); gold iridescent amber glass with iridescent scrollwork and panel decoration. (Fig. 50)

**286**

VASE, 1893-1920s
"2907 E L. C. Tiffany - Favrile" engraved on bottom
Tiffany Furnaces, Corona, Long Island, NY
2¾ x 3½ (dia); gold iridescent amber glass with green leaf-and-vine decoration. (Fig. 50)

**287**

VASE, 1893-1920s
"9121 M L. C. Tiffany - Inc - Favrile" engraved on bottom
Tiffany Furnaces, Corona, Long Island, NY
13¾ x 4½ (dia); gold iridescent vertical-rib patterned amber glass. (Fig. 50)

**288**

LAMP AND SHADE, 1893-1920s
"L. C. Tiffany - Favrile" on bottom of lamp
Tiffany Furnaces, Corona, Long Island, NY
Lamp: 14⅞ x 7½ (dia), shade: 4¾ x 9⅝ (dia); rib-molded shade with shaded iridescent wavy threads on greenish opalescent glass and amber glass base with greenish-gold iridescent wavy threads.

**289**

BOWL CENTERPIECE, 1893-1920s
"1561 L. C. Tiffany - Inc. Favrile" engraved on bottom
Tiffany Furnaces, Corona, Long Island, NY
2⅞ x 11 (dia); iridescent green-shaded amber glass with raised opalescent decoration in diaper pattern on outside and wheel-engraved floral decoration inside.

**290**

BOWL, 1893-1920s
"1561 L.C.T. Favrile" engraved on bottom
Tiffany Furnaces, Corona, Long Island, NY
2⅜ x 6¼ (dia); iridescent green-shaded amber glass with raised opalescent decoration in diaper pattern on outside.

**291**

SHERBET, 1893-1920s
"1281 L.C.T. Favrile" engraved on bottom
Tiffany Furnaces, Corona, Long Island, NY
3½ x 4½ (dia); iridescent blue-shaded opalescent glass.

**292**

BOWL, 1893-1920s
"1925 L.C.T. Favrile" engraved on bottom
Tiffany Furnaces, Corona, Long Island, NY
1¾ x 5¾ (dia); colorless glass with raised opalescent decoration in leafy-vine pattern and iridescent lining.

**293**

VASE, 1910s
"9452 H L. C. Tiffany - Favrile" engraved on bottom
Tiffany Furnaces, Corona, Long Island, NY
7¾ x 5¼ (dia); colorless glass with yellow, brown, and green foliate decoration applied to inner layers of thin opalescent and transparent ruby glass. (Fig. 51)

**294**
MORNING GLORY VASE, 1910s
"8060 L L. C. Tiffany Favrile" engraved on bottom
Tiffany Furnaces, Corona, Long Island, NY
6¼ x 4⅜ (dia); green-tinted glass encasing blue morning glories with mottled green leaves and yellow stems. (Fig. 52)

**295**
BUD VASE, 1893-1920s
"551 K L. C. Tiffany -Favrile" engraved on bottom
Tiffany Furnaces, Corona, Long Island, NY
7 x 3½ (dia); translucent red glass over white lining with blue to black outer casing drawn up to neck in six points.

**296**
BUD VASE, 1893-1920s
"3049 K L. C. Tiffany - Favrile" engraved on bottom
Tiffany Furnaces, Corona, Long Island, NY
12 x 4 (dia); translucent red glass with faint purple vertical threads. (Cover)

**297**
PAIR OF VASES, 1928-1931
"544 NASH" engraved on bottom of each
A. Douglas Nash, Tiffany Furnaces, Corona, Long Island, NY
4⅛ x 3 (dia); gold iridescent amber glass with molded base and crimped top.

## UNION GLASS COMPANY GLASS

**298**
VASE, 1893-1924
Attributed to Union Glass Company, Somerville, MA
6⅝ x 4¾ (dia); translucent white glass with green and iridescent gold pulled feather decoration and iridescent gold lining, flared top. (Fig. 47)

**299**
VASE, 1893-1924
"KEW-BLAS" mark in green on bottom
Union Glass Company, Somerville, MA
9⅛ x 4⅛ (dia); translucent white glass with green and iridescent gold pulled feather decoration and iridescent gold lining, flared top and base. (Fig. 47)

**300**
PAIR OF CHAMPAGNE GLASSES, 1893-1924
"KEW-BLAS" engraved on bottom of each
Union Glass Company, Somerville, MA
5 x 3⅜ (dia); gold iridescent amber glass.

**301**
PAIR OF FOOTED BOWLS, 1893-1924
"KEW-BLAS" engraved on bottom of each
Union Glass Company, Somerville, MA
3⅝ x 4⅞ (dia); gold iridescent amber glass.

**302**
STANDING SALT, early 20th century
"KEW-BLAS" engraved on bottom
Union Glass Company, Somerville, MA
3 x 3¼ (dia); gold iridescent amber glass.

**303**
PAIR OF CORDIAL GLASSES, 1893-1924
"KEW-BLAS" engraved on bottom of each
Union Glass Company, Somerville, MA
4½ x 2½ (dia); gold iridescent amber glass.

**304**
SET OF FOUR FINGERBOWLS AND PLATES, 1893-1924
"KEW-BLAS / A / 500" engraved on bottom
Union Glass Company, Somerville, MA
Bowl: 2 x 5 (dia), plate: ½ x 6⅝ (dia); gold iridescent amber glass.

**305**
SALT OR NUT DISH, 1893-1924
"KEW-BLAS" engraved on bottom
Union Glass Company, Somerville, MA
1⅛ x 3½ (dia); gold iridescent amber glass with scalloped rim.

**306**
SALT OR NUT DISH, 1893-1924
"KEW-BLAS" engraved on bottom
Union Glass Company, Somerville, MA
1 x 3 (dia); gold iridescent amber glass with scalloped rim.

**307**
PAIR OF GLASSES, 1893-1924
"KEW-BLAS" engraved on bottom
Union Glass Company, Somerville, MA
5 x 3¼ (dia); gold iridescent amber glass with four push-ins.

**308**
FLORIFORM VASE, 1893-1924
"KEW-BLAS" engraved on bottom
Union Glass Company, Somerville, MA
12¼ x 5¼ (dia); gold iridescent amber glass.

**309**
VASE, 1893-1924
"KEW-BLAS" engraved on bottom
Union Glass Company, Somerville, MA
6 x 4¾ (dia); vertical-rib patterned gold iridescent amber glass with scalloped top.

**310**
VASE, 1893-1924
"KEW-BLAS" engraved on bottom
Union Glass Company, Somerville, MA
8 x 6⅞ x 4⅛; vertical-rib patterned gold iridescent amber glass with wide rim.

**311**
SET OF FOUR TUMBLERS, 1893-1924
"KEW-BLAS" engraved on bottom
Union Glass Company, Somerville, MA
3⅜ x 2⅞ (dia); vertical-rib patterned gold iridescent amber glass with flaring base.

**312**
PAIR OF WINE GLASSES, 1893-1924
"KEW-BLAS" engraved on bottom
Union Glass Company, Somerville, MA
6¼ x 2⅞ (dia); gold iridescent amber glass.

**313**
VASE, 1893-1924
"KEW-BLAS" engraved on bottom
Union Glass Company, Somerville, MA
2¼ x 3 (dia); gold iridescent amber glass with scalloped top
(possibly cut from larger vase).

**314**
LAMP BASE AND SHADE, early 20th century
Probably Union Glass Company, Somerville, MA
15 x 10 (dia); colorless glass with outer casing of ruby glass
cut in medallions, fans, thumbprints, and other motifs.
(Fig. 46)

## QUEZAL ART GLASS

**315**
VASE, early 20th century
"QUEZAL / 870" engraved on bottom
Quezal Art Glass and Decorating Company, Brooklyn, NY
6½ x 5⅜ (dia); translucent white glass with green and iridescent gold pulled feather decoration and iridescent gold
lining, scalloped top. (Fig. 47)

**316**
VASE, early 20th century
Tiffany paper label on bottom (spurious)
Probably Quezal Art Glass and Decorating Company,
Brooklyn, NY
8 x 4¾ (dia); ribbed colorless glass cased with pale yellow
shaded translucent white glass with green iridescent scrolled
panels outlined in purple shaded iridescence.

**317**
PAIR OF LAMP SHADES, early 20th century
"Quezal" engraved on neck
Quezal Art Glass and Decorating Company, Brooklyn, NY
5 x 3½ (dia); gold iridescent amber glass.

**318**
VASE, early 20th century
"Quezal" engraved on bottom
Quezal Art Glass and Decorating Company, Brooklyn, NY
9 x 4¾ (dia); gold iridescent amber glass with silver overlay
decoration. (Fig. 22)

## DURAND ART GLASS

**319**
VASE, 1924-1933
"DURAND" in silver on bottom
Durand Art Glass Company, Vineland, NJ
8½ x 6 (dia); colorless glass with opaque white and translucent blue pulled feather decoration and cobalt blue upper
portion. (Fig. 48)

**320**
WIDE-BRIMMED DEEP DISH, 1924-1933
"DURAND / 2605" in silver on bottom
Durand Art Glass Company, Vineland, NJ
1½ x 14½ (dia); iridescent cobalt blue glass.

**321**
CANDLESTICK, 1924-1933
"DURAND / 2044" in silver on bottom
Durand Art Glass Company, Vineland, NJ
2½ x 5 (dia); iridescent cobalt blue glass with gold irides-
cent amber glass base.

**322**
LAMP BASE, 1924-1933
Attributed to Durand Art Glass Company, Vineland, NJ
11⅞ x 7⅛ (dia); iridescent cobalt blue glass with applied
glass threads.

**323**
VASE, 1924-1933
"DURAND 187-6" in silver on bottom
Durand Art Glass Company, Vineland, NJ
6½ x 4¼ (dia); iridescent translucent yellow glass with blue
and green leaf-and-vine decoration.

## MISCELLANEOUS UNITED STATES GLASS

**324**
VASE
"IMPERIAL" quadrant mark on bottom
Imperial Glass Company, Bellaire, OH
6 x 4¾ (dia); iridescent frosted amber glass.

**325**
BOWL, 1901-1924
Possibly H. C. Fry Glass Company, Rochester, PA
3⅞ x 11¼ (dia); pale amber glass with controlled bubbles
and applied white threads on scalloped rim.

**326**
BOWL, 1901-1924
Possibly H. C. Fry Glass Company, Rochester, PA
2 x 11¾ (dia); amber glass with random bubbles.

**327**
PAIR OF GOBLETS, 1901-1924
Attributed to H. C. Fry Glass Company, Rochester, PA
6¼ x 3½ (dia); colorless glass with applied pale-blue
threads around base of bowl.

**328**
BOWL, late 19th century
Probably Midwestern United States
3½ x 8 x 8; pink shaded to colorless glass with raised opalescent decoration in floral pattern, ruffled top in four large
scallops.

**329**
PAIR OF TRUMPET VASES, 1890-1925
Possibly Pairpoint Glass Works, New Bedford, MA, or
Union Glass Company, Somerville, MA
11⅜ x 5¼ (dia); ruby and colorless glass.

**330**
COVERED SUGAR BOWL, late 19th century
United States
6½ x 4⅛ (dia); mold-blown ruby glass with raised foliate
decoration on bulbous vertical ribs, silver-plated lid.

**331**
COVERED GINGER JAR, 1890-1920
Probably Midwestern United States or England
9¼ x 6¼ (dia); mold-blown silver-deposit ruby glass.

**332**
TWO-HANDLED BOX (missing cover), late 19th century
"WAVE CREST" trade mark stamped in red on bottom
C. F. Monroe Company, Meriden, CT
2⅜ x 6¾ x 5; molded painted opal glass with gilded metal mounts.

**333**
BOX (missing cover), late 19th century
"WAVE CREST" trade mark stamped in red on bottom
C. F. Monroe Company, Meriden, CT
1¾ x 4¼ (dia); molded painted opal glass with gilded metal mounts.

**334**
BOWL, late 19th century
Attributed to C. F. Monroe Company, Meriden, CT
2⅜ x 4 (dia); molded painted opal glass in matte finish.
(Fig. 45)

**335**
BOX WITH HINGED COVER, late 19th century
"WAVE CREST" trade mark stamped in red on bottom
C. F. Monroe Company, Meriden, CT
2¾ x 3¼ (dia); molded painted opal glass with gilded metal mounts. (Fig. 45)

**336**
BOX WITH HINGED COVER, late 19th century
"WAVE CREST" trade mark stamped in red on bottom
C. F. Monroe Company, Meriden, CT
3⅝ x 4 (dia); molded painted opal glass with gilded metal mounts. (Fig. 45)

**337**
BOX WITH HINGED COVER, late 19th century
Attributed to C. F. Monroe Company, Meriden, CT
3½ x 5 (dia); molded painted opal glass with gilded metal mounts and silk liner. (Fig. 45)

**338**
JAR, late 19th century
Rampant lion trade mark stamped in red on bottom
Smith Brothers, New Bedford, MA
5¼ x 6¼ (dia); molded painted opal glass in matte finish.
(Fig. 45)

**339**
VASE, 1880-1890
Probably Hobbs, Brockunier & Company, Wheeling, WV
7¼ x 4⅛; orange-pink spangled glass with white lining, crimped top, and applied colorless tooled glass handles.
(Fig. 20)

**340**
ROSE BOWL, late 19th century
Probably Hobbs, Brockunier & Company, Wheeling, WV
4¼ x 5¼ (dia); pink spangled glass with colorless glass lining and ruffled top. (Fig. 20)

**341**
FOOTED BOWL, late 19th century
Probably Midwestern United States
4½ x 6 (dia); mottled pink and brown cased over white with outer layer of colorless glass and five applied colorless glass feet.

**342**
PICKLE CASTOR, late 19th century
United States, or possibly Europe
12 x 4¾ x 4½; inverted-thumbprint patterned colorless glass with ruby lining and enamel and gilt decoration in silver-plated stand marked "Hartford Silver Plate Co" and tongs marked "Rogers Bros." Meriden, CT.

**343**
PAIR OF JACK-IN-THE-PULPIT VASES, early 20th century
United States or Europe
8¾ x 4¾ x 3¼; opalescent glass with green shaded and gilded ruffled rim.

**344**
RECTANGULAR TRAY, late 19th to early 20th century
United States
1⅛ x 8½ x 7⅛; opaque white cased over colorless glass with enamel and gilt floral decoration and cut central star.

**345**
COVERED SUGAR BOWL, 1880s
Probably Adams & Company, Pittsburgh, PA
6¾ x 4½ (dia); pressed ruby-stained colorless glass in Ruby-thumbprint pattern.

**346**
CELERY VASE, 1880s
Probably Adams & Company, Pittsburgh, PA
4½ x 4½ (dia); pressed ruby-stained colorless glass in Ruby-thumbprint pattern.

**347**
COVERED BUTTER DISH, 1880s
Probably Adams & Company, Pittsburgh, PA
5½ x 7½ (dia); pressed ruby-stained colorless glass in Ruby-thumbprint pattern.

**348**
PITCHER, 1880s
Probably Adams & Company, Pittsburgh, PA
8¼ x 5¾ x 4⅛; pressed ruby-stained colorless glass in Ruby-thumbprint pattern.

**349**
CREAMER, 1880s
Probably Adams & Company, Pittsburgh, PA
5 x 5 x 4⅛; pressed ruby-stained colorless glass in Ruby-thumbprint pattern.

**350**
SPOON HOLDER, 1880s
Probably Adams & Company, Pittsburgh, PA
4 x 3¾ (dia); pressed ruby-stained colorless glass in Ruby-thumbprint pattern.

## CUT AND ENGRAVED GLASS

**351**
VASE, late 19th century

Attributed to Stevens and Williams, Brierley Hill, England
10½ x 6 (dia); wheel-engraved colorless glass with birds and floral sprays, panel-cut stem with gilded filigree designs, and gilded rim. (Fig. 28)

**352**
VASE, late 19th century
"Geo Woodall" engraved in oval panel on side;
"THOMAS WEBB & SONS" acid stamp on bottom
George Woodall, Thomas Webb & Sons, Stourbridge, England
13 x 6⅝ (dia); cut and engraved colorless glass showing figure of Undine in oval medallion. (Fig. 29)

**353**
DECANTER, late 19th century
United States
10 x 4¾ (dia); cut colorless glass in hobstar, fan, and other motifs with sterling silver mounts by Gorham Manufacturing Co., Providence, RI.

**354**
PAIR OF COMPOTES, early 20th century
United States
6 x 7¾ (dia); colorless glass wheel-engraved in floral pattern.

**355**
CAKE STAND, late 19th to early 20th century
"Hawkes" fleur-de-lis with birds in trefoil acid stamp on bottom
T. G. Hawkes & Company, Corning, NY
2½ x 8¾ (dia); wheel engraved and cut colorless glass.

**356**
SYRUP, late 19th to early 20th century
"HAWKES" and trefoil acid stamp on bottom
T. G. Hawkes & Company, Corning, NY
6¾ x 4⅛ x 3⅛; colorless glass cut and engraved with iris blooms and leaves, sterling silver mounts. (Fig. 31)

**357**
TRUMPET VASE, late 19th to early 20th century
"HAWKES" and trefoil acid stamp on bottom
T. G. Hawkes & Company, Corning, NY
12 x 4⅝ (dia); colorless glass cut in panels with Greek key bands.

**358**
PAIR OF COMPOTES WITH FOOTED-CUP INSERTS, early 20th century
"HAWKES" acid stamp on bottom
T. G. Hawkes & Company, Corning, NY
Compote: 6½ x 5⅜ (dia), insert: 2⅞ x 3⅝ (dia); Steuben Verre de Soie (iridescent colorless glass) blanks decorated by Hawkes with wheel-engraved neo-classical motifs.

**359**
VASE, late 19th to early 20th century
"J. Hoare & Co. / 1853 / Corning" acid stamp on bottom
J. Hoare & Company, Corning, NY
12 x 4¾ (dia); colorless glass cut in hobstar and other motifs.

**360**
COMPOTE, 1888-1936
"Libbey" acid stamp on bottom

Libbey Glass Company, Toledo, OH
2½ x 6 (dia); colorless glass engraved in blackberry design.

**361**
COMPOTE, 1888-1936
"Libbey" acid stamp on bottom
Libbey Glass Company, Toledo, OH
4½ x 6¼; colorless glass cut and engraved in thumbprint and floral motifs.

**362**
COCKTAIL GLASS, 1888-1936
Attributed to Libbey Glass Company, Toledo, OH
4¾ x 3½; colorless glass with rough cut (unfinished) decoration.

**363**
PAIR OF COMPOTES, late 19th to early 20th century
England or Ireland
5½ x 9½ x 5¾; cut colorless glass.

**364**
COMPOTE, late 19th century
Probably England
9¼ x 9½ (dia); cut colorless glass. (Fig. 26)

**365**
COVERED COMPOTE, 19th century
Probably England or Ireland
12¾ x 7¼ (dia); colorless glass cut in thumbprint pattern. (Fig. 25)

**366**
EWER WITH STOPPER, late 19th to early 20th century
England or United States (Pittsburgh or Corning)
10¼ x 5¾ x 5 (dia); colorless glass cut in diamond and fan pattern with engraved "D" on side. (Fig. 27)

**367**
DECANTER WITH STOPPER, late 19th to early 20th century
England or United States (Pittsburgh or Corning)
10¼ x 5 (dia); colorless glass cut in diamond and fan pattern with engraved "D" on side. (Fig. 27)

**368**
TIERED EPERGNE CENTERPIECE, 19th century
Probably England
16½ x 13⅜ (dia); colorless glass cut in strawberry diamond pattern in Anglo-Irish style. (Fig. 24)

**369**
PAIR OF WATER GOBLETS, 19th century
Attributed to England or Ireland
5½ x 3½ (dia); colorless glass cut in diamond and panel design.

**370**
BOWL, 19th century
Probably Bohemia
3½ x 11 (dia); ruby-stained colorless glass cut and engraved in strawberry diamond pattern with floral border. (Fig. 30)

**371**
COMPOTE, 19th century
Probably Bohemia
6¼ x 7¼ (dia); ruby-stained colorless glass with enameled and gilded decoration and applied glass beads.

# Glass works and makers represented in the collection

Adams & Company, Pittsburgh, PA, 1861-1891 (succeeded by United States Glass Company)

Boston and Sandwich Glass Company, Sandwich, MA, 1825-1888

Frederick Carder, 1863-1963
worked at Stevens & Williams, Brierley Hill, England, 1880-1903
manager of Steuben Glass Works and successors, 1903-1932
Art Director of Corning Glass Works, 1932-1959

Durand Art Glass Company, Vineland, NJ, 1924-1933

Daum Frères, later Cristalleries de Nancy, Nancy, France, c. 1875 to date

H. C. Fry Glass Company, Rochester, PA, 1901-1924

Emile Gallé, 1846-1904
established first glass house in 1867
began art glass production in 1874, factory continued until 1913

Gundersen-Pairpoint (see Mount Washington Glass Company)

T. G. Hawkes & Company, Corning, NY, 1880-1962

J. Hoare & Company, Brooklyn, NY, c. 1857 - c. 1873; Corning, NY, c. 1873-1920

Hobbs, Brockunier & Company, Wheeling, WV, 1861 - c. 1890 (successor to Barnes-Hobbs & Company, established in 1845)

Imperial Glass Company, Bellaire, OH, c. 1901 to date

Libbey Glass Company (see New England Glass Company)

Joseph Locke, 1846-1936
worked at various English glass houses until 1882
worked at New England Glass Company and successors, 1882-1891
established Locke Art Glass Company, Pittsburgh, PA, in 1891

Johanne Loetz, Klosternmuhle, Austria, c. 1840-1848
Johanne Loetz Witwe and successors 1848-c. 1914

C. F. Monroe Company, Meriden, CT, dates unknown

Mount Washington Glass Company, 1837-1957
Mount Washington Glass Works, later Company, South Boston, later New Bedford, MA, 1837-1894
The Pairpoint Glass Works, New Bedford, MA, 1894-1938
The Gundersen Glass Works, New Bedford, MA, 1938-1952
The Gundersen-Pairpoint Glass Works, New Bedford, MA, 1952-1957

A. Douglas Nash (see Tiffany)

New England Glass Company, East Cambridge, MA, 1818-1888
New England Glass Works, Wm. Libbey & Son, Props., 1878-1888
Libbey Glass Company, Toledo, OH, 1888-1936
Owens-Illinois, Inc. 1936 to date

Quezal Art Glass and Decorating Company, Brooklyn, NY, c. 1902-1925

Steuben Glass Works, Corning, NY, 1903-1918
Stueben Division of Corning Glass Works, Corning, NY, 1918-1933
Steuben Glass, Inc., 1933 to date

Stevens & Williams, Ltd. (now Royal Brierley Crystal), Brierley Hill, Staffordshire, England, 1847 to date

Louis C. Tiffany, 1848-1933
Tiffany Furnaces, Corona, Long Island, NY, 1892-1928
Tiffany Studios, New York, NY, 1900-1919
Tiffany Furnaces operated by A. Douglas Nash, 1928-1931

Union Glass Company, Somerville, MA, 1854-1924
"KEW-BLAS" name first used in 1893

Thomas Webb & Sons, Stourbridge, England, 1837-1964

Thomas Woodall, 1849-1926; and George Woodall, 1850-1925
worked at J. & J. Northwood until c. 1874
worked at Thomas Webb & Sons, c. 1874-1911